A NEW THEORY OF VALUE / The Canadian economics of H.A. Innis

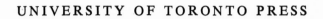

UNIVERSITY OF TORONTO PRESS

A new theory of value

The Canadian economics of H.A. Innis

Robin Neill

© University of Toronto Press 1972
Toronto and Buffalo
Printed in Canada
ISBN 0-8020-1855-6 cloth
ISBN 0-8020-6152-4 paper
Microfiche ISBN 0-8020-0182-3
LC 77-185867

Contents

Preface

This little book, which can hardly lay claim to being more than an essay, is one distillate of a larger study of economic thought in Canada. In its original form it covered much more of Innis' work and included a good deal of biographical material. All of that, together with the larger study of economic thought, was required initially to provide the proper perspectives for judging the doctrinal content of Innis' work and its place in the broad tradition of western economic literature. Once that judgment was made it became possible to segregate and reduce the contextual material. It is hoped that what is left will provide a suitable companion volume to D.G. Creighton's biography, *Harold Adams Innis: Portrait of a Scholar*, and a beginning for the second volume of Craufurd Goodwin's *Canadian Economic Thought*.

To those who are familiar with the work of Marshall McLuhan I should say that I have explained Innis lineally from the point of view of economics. I have translated him back into the world of print for the benefit of the economists who have never left that world. To them I should say that this is a critique of value theory as an instrument for understanding economic progress, and an attempt to show how Innis tried a fresh approach in that regard.

At different stages in the preparation of this work I have been helped by Professor W.T. Easterbrook of the University of Toronto,

and by Professor J.J. Spengler and the late Professor R.S. Smith of
Duke University. I am grateful to the Innis family for giving me
access to unpublished material, some of which I have incorporated
in an appendix, and for their patience with my stumbling. In some
way the work is a tribute to the men with whom I have lived. Their
tolerance is the hallmark of their Christianity.

This book has been published with the help of a grant from the
Social Science Research Council of Canada, using funds provided
by the Canada Council.

Charlottetown, January 1972   ROBIN NEILL

A NEW THEORY OF VALUE / The Canadian economics of H.A. Innis

Introduction

The appearance in the last few years of numerous attempts to establish the validity of the staples thesis of Canadian history is evidence of a need to review and assess the work of Harold Innis. It is some time since the name of Innis was the shibboleth of erudition in Canadian economics, and it may be that there is now sufficient historical distance to make possible an objective appraisal of his contribution. In the heyday of his academic popularity his name was used to decorate all types of discourse in such a way as to obscure not only the weaknesses of the arguments of the protagonist but even the strength of the arguments of Innis. For one who was a student at that time, such confusion needs to be cleared up. There are, however, more pressing reasons for attempting a précis of Innis' thought. The naïve Keynesianism and simplistic price theory against which he protested have proven to be of little help in understanding the Canadian case. In fact they may have exacerbated the problems they were intended to solve, for in some respects those problems are more with us today than they were even in Innis' time.

Beginning with the foundation laid by Thorstein Veblen and accepting Veblen's criticism of both the classical and neoclassical economic doctrines, Innis elaborated a theory of growth applicable to a marginal or hinterland economy. Having begun with Veblen, he was not content with the merely formal categories and logical machinations of traditional theory. He extended his work to the explanation of why, in addition to how, growth had taken place. This took him well beyond the rehearsed lines of the usual theorizing, but it did not lead him into a diffuse and eclectic approach. Economic growth was Innis' concern and all economic phenomena were explained from that point of view. From start to finish Innis moved in search of the laws of growth and decline.

Both price theory and capital theory of the generally accepted sort owe a heavy debt to nineteenth-century rationalism and, therefore, they exhibit its weaknesses. Rationalism, the so-called utilitarian ethic, is in fact no ethic at all. It is an attempt to obviate ethics by placing the logic of choice where value judgment ought to be. In consequence, both price and growth theories fail to provide any guidance as to why events occur or whether they are good or bad. What is described in the case of rationalist growth theory is the process that takes place *as growth is happening*; but why growth takes place, why it takes place at a certain rate, or whether it is a good thing, are questions quite beyond the scope of that form of enquiry. In the case of price theory what is described is either the logical consistency of inter-related prices or the process by which that consistency is achieved; but why prices are ultimately what they are, or whether what they are is good, is again quite beyond the scope of the enquiry. Innis was concerned with the forces of technology and value judgment that ultimately determine prices and the extent to which growth takes place. For this reason, though he was unaware of it, he shared with J.M. Keynes the experience of freedom from the hoax of nineteenth-century hedonism.

Innis did not ignore the traditional type of growth theory. Far from it, for a knowledge of the implications of technical constraints and values requires the tracing down of their logical ramification throughout the economic system. His aim was to ensure that prices and quantification be given content and meaning. What we have in Innis' work, therefore, is the elaboration of an historical theory of growth, focusing on the efficient and final causes of what has or has had existence, rather than on the formal and instrumental processes constituting logically consistent models that do not exist and never have existed except in the mind. Using this distinction, then, it may be said that Innis, along with others, began the construction of an 'existentialist' economics, thus providing a necessary complement to the rationalist economics of the previous century.

Appearances notwithstanding, the work of men like Innis and Keynes has not been lost on subsequent generations of scholars. Certainly the theory of economic depression as outlined by Keynes has received general acceptance and, in Canada, Innis' historical work has had a wide influence. Even more than this, however, the philosophical presumptions that form the spirit of their work have not been forgotten, although this is seldom recognized. Keynes himself did not think that the succeeding generation had managed to maintain its liberation from the intellectual trap of rationalism; but the widespread acceptance of the pure positivist approach with its concomitant disassociation from any value judgment whatsoever is fair evidence to the contrary. Pure positivism has taken the discipline of economics into the realm of the merely instrumental. Increasingly, the so-designated economist finds himself in the role of the technician, the clerk, and the administrator. This has freed policy and the economics of policy from the bias of formal models and ancient theory. It is not that economists are consciously elaborating an 'existentialist' economics, but in fact much of that body of knowledge which was once contained under the umbrella of economics is now existentialist as defined above.

It may be that the intellectual presuppositions of an era become evident only when they appear in sharp contrast to some alternative. This will happen only at the beginning and at the end of the era. Thus statements of the presuppositions of our own day can only be found in the literature of the preceding transitional period. In so far as Veblen, Innis and Keynes are representative of that period, their positions, though not evidently so, are now generally accepted. Though all the paraphernalia of the nineteenth century theory remains in circulation, to the point that one is tempted to believe that nothing has happened since, its underpinning in judgment and preconception has changed so that its entire content and meaning is not what it was before. This last point requires more elaboration, but that might lead to the writing of the book in its introduction. I leave any further discussion of it to the appropriate points in the text.

So far, I have attempted to introduce the reader to what I have
to say about Innis' thought. The second part of this introduction
deals with how I try to say it. The book is something of a Dagwood
sandwich. A core account of Innis' work is sandwiched between
chapters which attempt to place it in the general stream of western
economic thought. This main sandwich is then set between two
other chapters sketching the Canadian context of Innis' work.
These, the outer slices of bread, are composed of biographical
material and gleanings from the gossip that is the history of economic thought in Canada.

A reader who is interested only in the doctrinal content of Innis'
work may begin reading at chapter three and conclude with chapter
eight. This is the core section, the argument of which is continuous
from start to finish. Chapter three sets out the empirical data as
Innis saw them in the historical case of Canada. Historians and those
who think of Innis in relation to the staples thesis of Canadian
development should find this chapter most interesting. Chapter four
elaborates Innis' interpretation of the data. Although it has been
impossible to separate completely fact and theory into these two
chapters, to a large extent chapter four does contain an undiluted
statement of Innis' theory of economic progress. That chapter,
therefore, is already a partial conclusion to the argument. Nonetheless, one major problem, the problem of values in economic theory,
remained unsolved at this point in the evolution of Innis' thought.
Chapter five narrates his reappraisal of the Canadian scene as the
answer to that problem emerged. The remaining three chapters of
this section are a précis of what Innis thought to be the implications
of his answer for the theory of economic growth, the history of
economic thought, and economic history, respectively. The last two
of these chapters will be of greatest interest to those who would like
to explore the intellectual roots of the doctrine of Marshall Mc-
Luhan.

The sandwich to the core section, chapters two and nine, deal
specifically with Innis' place in the history of economic thought.
Nonetheless, the historian of economic thought should read chapters
four and five as well if he is to get the whole argument. He should
also bear in mind that it is clearly impossible to write a history of

economic thought in such a short space. Only a mythologized account, some sort of snapshot of the development, is possible. Further, the weaknesses of a brief treatment are compounded in the present case by the fact that the aim is to expose contentious and problematic areas of the science. The result is a simple interpretation of the history of economic thought, tailored to a particular task. Chapter two purports to raise the problems of economics as Innis received them and chapter nine attempts to state Innis' resolution of them.

Finally we come to the outer layers of the multiple sandwich and the Canadian context of Innis' work. Chapter one is largely biographical, but by no means competes with Donald Creighton's book.[1] It simply presents those elements in Innis' story that best provide a background for his economic doctrine. For this reason it turns slightly towards a history of economic thought in Canada. The last chapter, being something of an account of the impact of Innis' work, turns very markedly in that same direction.

That is the book. I make no apologies for my failure to recreate the sense of romance and mystery that is part of Innis' essays on communications and of the work of Marshall McLuhan. Much of that intriguing charm is a consequence of wit and art. It falls in fair measure under the head of poetics and aesthetics. I have attempted only the less exciting but still important task of spelling out their prosaic, intellectual content. The values that constitute society are a set of judgments that, to a significant degree, are structured by the dominant means of transportation and communication. That is to say, the medium is the message; and the rest is a witty and artful elaboration of this.

1 *Harold Adams Innis: Portrait of a Scholar* (Toronto, 1957).

1

Harold Adams Innis

Harold Adams Innis was born in 1894 on a small farm in southern Ontario. When he was eleven he was admitted to what is now called grade nine in the Otterville high school. Two years later, in the fall of 1908, he began commuting twenty miles to the Woodstock Collegiate Institute. After graduating, the young Innis taught for a year and then registered at McMaster University. With the exception of one summer, when he took a teaching position in rural Manitoba, his thoughts from 1912 to 1916 were dominated by undergraduate interests, studies, and debating. He enlisted immediately after the spring convocation, 1916, and by Christmas his group, the 69th Battery of the Canadian Army, was on the front in France. By the end of July he had been wounded and sent to England for convalescence. In the spring of 1918 he arrived back in Canada, passed the examination required for an MA in economics at McMaster and registered for the summer term at the University of Chicago.

As prosaic as all of this was, and normal for someone in Innis' position at the time, he himself did not accept it as such. Years later he explained his own point of view.

After eight months of the mud and lice and rats of France in which much of the time was spent cursing government officials in Ottawa I have without doubt developed an abnormal slant. I have never had the slightest interest since that time in people who were helping in the war with a job in Ottawa or London. The contrast between their method of living and France made it simply impossible for me to regard them as having anything to do with the war and I continue to look on them with contempt. This of course is unreasonable but there it is. When I came back in the spring of 1918 to do graduate work I found the universities depleted of staff in Canada and at Chicago in the United States because people were bustling back and forth winning the war, they said, or their friends said. This means of course that after taking the dirt in France I was expected to take more dirt when I came back from people whom I regarded with contempt.[1]

Innis' somewhat misanthropic attitude had roots farther back than his experiences in the war and extended itself beyond that special situation to the peacetime civil service. In part it grew out of severe penury throughout his student life and out of the need to move to progressively larger centres to advance his education. It was aggravated by the damage done in these circumstances to his academic progress, and further aggravated by the effects of the war. In 1916 no examinations were necessary for students who volunteered for military service. Although Innis insisted on writing anyway, the arrangement did not increase his confidence in the meaning of his degree. Then he acquired his Master's degree by correspondence through Khaki College, and disappointment over what he learned in that instance led him to further studies in economics at Chicago, where, in many ways, things were not much better. Again lack of money forced him to take on work not directly connected with his studies and the lingering effects of his injury hampered him. So evident were his problems that his director warned him some time before his final examinations that he was not in good physical condition and that he ought not to study more than two hours each day. In fact he failed one of the subjects in those examinations and was convinced that his being given the degree in 1920 was just 'further evidence of the kindness of people at Chicago.' His 'uneasy conscience' as he called it, continued to lead him on to further studies but it also engendered a certain lack of confidence that came to the

1 Letter from H.A. Innis to A.H. Cole (Aug. 8, 1943).

surface in his impatience with facile sophistry and pure intellectual panache.

Innis' strong religious background in the Scottish, Baptist tradition made a contribution to this incipient anarchism.[2] It is true that despite considerable social pressure he refused to accept the ministry that his family had planned for him, and even refused baptism. Nonetheless he passed too many years in sheltered religious surroundings not to have absorbed some of the preconceptions and problems of the doctrine involved. During his time at McMaster there was serious dispute over the Modernist position and Innis took his side with Professor Ten Broeke whom he considered 'by far the most heretical thinker in the University'; but that debate did not touch on the entrenched doctrines of individualism in matters of conscience and separation of church and state. These specific elements of the Baptist faith remained with Innis throughout his life.[3]

There were, of course, other formative influences during the years at McMaster.

One of those of whom I was most enthusiastic must be mentioned, Mr W.S. Wallace, lecturer in history and later Librarian of the University of Toronto. He had returned fresh from Oxford, had retained his Canadian accent and dealt with the general subject of history, and in particular with Canadian history, with enthusiasm and effect. I can still remember his statements that 'liberty is impossible without order,' that 'the economic interpretation of history is not the only interpretation but it is the deepest interpretation.' ... Perhaps one of the most striking teachers was Professor James Ten Broeke of philosophy ... He opened the subject of philosophy in such a way as to free those who sought to be free from the conventions of philosophical thought ... At that time McMaster was not in a position to pay large salaries and young men were appointed as a rule. Perhaps the most aggressive of those was W.J. Donald who lectured in political economy ... His youth and enthusiasm attracted students and led me to select economics as my chief field of interest.[4]

2 H.G. Johnson, one time student of Innis, on being questioned about Innis' attitude stated that Innis was an anarchist. (Personal interview, Feb. 1966.)
3 On being questioned about Innis' attitude V.W. Bladen simply replied that Innis was a Baptist. (Personal interview, Sept. 1954.)
4 'Autobiography,' 35–6.

W.J.A. Donald himself had graduated from McMaster in 1909 and had gone on to post-graduate studies at the University of Chicago. In 1913 he returned to Canada with a Canadian topic for his PH D dissertation and a lectureship at his *alma mater*. Within two years, while Innis was his student, Donald published four articles and his only book, *The Canadian Iron and Steel Industry*. Clearly he had enthusiasm, and to this Innis attributed his own academic success. 'The effects of my enthusiasm,' he wrote, 'can perhaps be suggested in the fact that I won the D.E. Thomson Scholarship in Economics and the Teitzel Prize in Philosophy ... in the examinations for 1915.'[5] The character of this mutual enthusiasm may be illustrated by a citation from the article Donald published in that same year. 'Canada's fiscal system, a child of political expediency, has been reared by a grasping father, the manufacturers, and a subservient mother, the politicians.'[6] Further evidence of the strength and 'radical' character of Donald's influence on Innis is provided by the tone of the student's own first years of lecturing when he was withdrawn from teaching a course in Canadian economic history, in part because he developed the subject 'along too radical lines.'[7]

The Canadian Iron and Steel Industry was Donald's doctoral dissertation. It was prepared under the direction of C.W. Wright who was personally interested in opening up the subject of economic development in Canada. Indeed it was in view of Wright's interest that the iron and steel industry had been chosen, since it was presumed that development of that industry was a necessary basis for any development of the economy as a whole. The dissertation proved this assumption false. Repeated references to the fact that the industry was most successful 'in the finishing stages' rather than the primary stages indicated Donald's conviction that in the Canadian case iron and steel was a dependent element in the development process. Through Donald's influence Innis, in turn, undertook a dissertation under C.W. Wright at Chicago. In Innis' case the topic suggested by Wright, the Canadian Pacific Railway, was a better point of departure for exploring the course of Canadian history.

5 'Autobiography,' 36.
6 'Canadian Financial Problems.'
7 'Autobiography,' 88.

Innis did not make up his mind about his career until after he had been at Chicago for some time, but circumstances there were such that when he did decide to go on in economics he did so with considerable personal commitment. Part of this was the result of an intense nationalism which he shared with many Canadians after the first world war. Part was the result of some fortunate aspects of his post-graduate training. There was at that time considerable dissent in the United States with respect to the tenets of neoclassical theory. The most fundamental assumptions of economics were being questioned by men like Thorstein Veblen and John R. Commons, and the success of their attack on accepted doctrine was forcing radical new departures. While some of this was brought to Innis' attention through the influence of men like C.W. Wright and C.S. Duncan, his most effective contact was made through Frank Knight who was then an instructor in statistics at Chicago. Knight's scepticism captivated the angry young veteran and drew him into a small, informal group that gathered to discuss the work of Thorstein Veblen.[8]

Innis returned to Canada in 1920 to take a position in the department of political economy at the University of Toronto. It was a good time to arrive. With the exception of its redoubtable head, James Mavor, the department was young and aware that it had the economics of Canada still to discover. Mavor had attempted an introduction to Canadian economic history but had left it unfinished. C.R. Fay, the economic historian, was in Toronto in those years and was aware that something new might happen. He and Innis became life-long friends in their mutual endeavour to see that it did. V.W. Bladen, recently arrived from Oxford, was pulled into the effort by Innis' insistence that he could not possibly understand the economics of Canada unless he personally visited every part of it. Innis took that medicine himself. The two senior academic economists in Canada who could have helped were James Mavor and Adam Shortt. Mavor was an impressive personality but after his study condemning public ownership in hydroelectric power Innis concluded that he had sold out to the vested interests. Adam Shortt,

8 The group included F.H. Knight, Carter Goodrich, Morris Copeland,
   W.B. Smith, J.W. Angell, at least. See Innis' 'Autobiography,' 8.

though not at the University of Toronto, was of much help and at one time Innis began to collect a bibliography of Shortt's works in an attempt to establish the then current state of Canadian economics. That stopped when Shortt published a history of currency and finance as an introduction to Canadian economics; Innis rejected the work because, he said, it sided with the price economists. It may be that Oscar Skelton, by that time a senior civil servant, was the only one who gave the necessary leads. Skelton had been an outstanding student of Veblen and had applied Veblen's ideas in a partial economic history of Canada. In a practical sense the greatest help came from Innis' former history professor, W.S. Wallace, who had become librarian of the University of Toronto. Wallace was editor of the *Canadian Historical Review* to which Innis contributed his bibliographical work in Canadian economics.

The prodigious effort Innis made to compile a bibliography of Canadian economics failed in its main intent. It did provide a much needed publication of what was then being done in Canada. It further provided evidence of Innis' belief in the existence of Canadian economics, if not of its actual existence, and it was an indication of his strong desire to make a contribution in that regard. Despite the failure of the bibliographical research he did make his contribution by taking the characteristic position of a long line of Canadian nationalist economists, most of whom remained unknown to him.[9] But that too was characteristic in that stream of thought, for it was the persistence of the Canadian problem rather than the public success and notoriety of its exponents that formed the basis of continuity.

Throughout the nineteenth century it was evident to some in Canada that the economics of *laissez-faire* had been developed in relation to conditions in an advanced, metropolitan centre and was a rationalization of activities that would be beneficial from that point of view. Canada was a young, hinterland country and policies of rational allocation in the international economy had no necessary connection with Canada's relative or absolute growth. Accordingly,

9 Some account of Canadian economics before Innis can be found in Craufurd Goodwin's *Canadian Economic Thought* and in R.F. Neill, 'Social Credit and National Policy in Canada,' *Journal of Canadian Studies*, 3 (1968), 3–13.

men like Robert Gourlay, E.G. Wakefield, and John Rae, like
Isaac Buchanan, J.B. Hurlbert, and John McLean, and like the
members of the National Currency school took pains to point out
the peculiar difficulties of the Canadian case and the radical weakness of Cosmopolitan economics in meeting them. Some evidence
of their success can be found in the adoption of the National Policy
of 1878, even though the success of the National Policy in its turn
entailed the confusion of their position.

The effects of the National Policy were not uniform throughout
Canada since some regions developed metropolitan characteristics
with respect to others. In consequence, the sort of economics that
had been accepted in the genesis of the National Policy became
unacceptable to the dominant regions in the rationalization of internal policies. In fact that region which had produced the strongest
statements of the nationalist position and which had been most
active in the attempt to raise Canada from the position of a colonial
frontier found itself with frontiers of its own, both to the west and
to the east, and with a vested interest in keeping those frontier areas
in an economically subordinate position. The resulting change in
attitude is strikingly evident in a comparison of the general positions
of John Rae and Adam Shortt. Rae, writing in the eighteen-twenties
and thirties, made a forthright and successful attack on the work of
Adam Smith, therein presenting the position and economics of the
frontier as opposed to the rationalization of policies suited to established centres of development. Together with Isaac Buchanan he
took the position that government control of credit was superior to
the automatic gold standard system, and he worked to prevent Lord
Sydenham and his disciple, Francis Hincks, from enacting for
Canada the gold standard policies of the Currency school. By 1930
Upper Canada, represented by Adam Shortt, was supporting the
doctrines of the Currency school in the face of protests coming
from the prairies. By 1930 the Social Crediters of western Canada
were taking a position with respect to the St Lawrence Basin similar
to that taken in 1830 by the St Lawrence Basin with respect to
England. Consequently when Innis turned to Adam Shortt to discover the position of Canadian economics he was faced with a situation in which the economics of internal conflict was obfuscating

the economics of the country as a whole. It was significant that he rejected Shortt's work because it sided with the price economists.

There were, of course, additional complications deriving from the peculiarities of the Canadian case. Over the turn of the century, when the growth of Canada was bringing about industrialization, the beginnings of the welfare state, expansion of the school system and the general advance of democracy, academic economics became generally acceptable for the first time. As a young country, Canada was forced to build up its universities by importing people who had been educated in advanced countries and, consequently, in the economics of metropolitan centres. Not only were these people ignorant of the Canadian case, but they were predisposed by training to misunderstand it. All things considered, therefore, it is not surprising that Innis was forced into a fresh start in the development of Canadian economics.

Thus the first fifteen years at Toronto were a difficult but fruitful time in Innis' career, involving a remarkable effort that was crowned with success in 1930 when he published his own introduction to Canadian economics in the form of a history of the fur trade. About that same time, as he took a more prominent position in the department, his academic ambitions became confused with departmental politics, adding a measure of personal upset to his burden. Then the depression came with its untold misery creating intense demands for economists to explain the problem and produce adequate remedies. In 1929, following the crash, the Canadian Political Science Association was revitalized. Innis was soon drawn into the organizational effort. Only a year before, with the help of the Bladens, he had begun to publish a periodical, *Contributions to Canadian Economics*. It provided the necessary medium for the CPSA and its success in that capacity was a major factor in the Association's decision to launch the *Canadian Journal of Economics and Political Science* in 1935. All this involvement had its rewards and its price. In 1934 he was elected fellow of the Royal Society of Canada. In 1936 he was promoted to professor of political economy and elected vice-president of the Canadian Political Science Association, but shortly before his subsequent appointment as head of the department of political economy at Toronto and his later election as president of the Association he suffered a 'break-down' and was forced into a long period of rest.

Not the least of Innis' troubles were the difficulties of the department of political economy. In 1928 E.J. Urwick, fresh from England and unaware of the situation in Toronto, succeeded R.M. McIver as head. When, in one or two departmental seminars, Innis elaborated some Veblenesque ideas about the necessity of an objective and scientific approach Urwick wrote him off as just another fact-grubbing, materialistic American. Subsequently Urwick attempted to by-pass Innis by promoting Hubert Kempt to the rank of associate professor. The conflict that ensued was bitter and involved Innis' resignation until Urwick was prevailed upon to promote him too. Again in 1934 the rancour of the incident broke out in the form of a dispute over the role of values in social science. The matter had been an important one for Veblen and two of Innis' teachers, Frank Knight and J.M. Clark, had been involved in a serious dispute over it while he was at Chicago. Innis retained his contact with Knight and seems to have come close to him in 1934 when he again opened up the topic of values at the meetings of the American Economic Association. Actually there were fair grounds for agreement between Innis and Urwick but in the closeness of that intra-departmental dispute points of agreement were blurred if not lost sight of altogether.

Once he himself became head, Innis' troubles in the department soon began to look much like those of his predecessor. His attitude changed and he and Urwick corresponded amiably for two or three years before the latter's death. But it took much more than the mere change in the headship to bring about reconciliation. The depression brought on a new economics and led to the second world war. The approach of war, in turn, had its effect on economics in Canada. As autarchy grew in Europe, United States' interest and capital turned to opportunities in the Americas. A series of Canadian-American conferences, increases in research funds from United States' sources and the earlier entry of Canada into the war made Innis acutely aware of the increasing economic centralization of North America without adequate political adjustment. In his concern about the general breakdown of order, and frightened by the rape of the universities during the war, he took a closer look at the sort of world in which the United States was emerging as the economic and political pace-setter. His intense nationalism was aroused and he began to regard Canada, a marginal area in French, British, and American empires, as one of the last strongholds of western civilization. If Gibbon wrote *The Decline and Fall of the Roman Empire* about Britain and not about Rome, as Innis said he had; then in the same sense, Innis wrote his history of communications about Canada and not about Egypt, Greece, and Europe.

In the midst of the war and the troubles it caused in the university the old question of values again came to the fore. Sociology was just then breaking away from political economy at Toronto and once more there was unnerving debate about the scientific character of social science. This time Innis took the side of ancient tradition against the purely 'scientific' approach, and with considerable success.

Success in the debate over sociology followed from the fact that Innis was generally a success as head of the department of political economy, controlling its progress and somehow eliciting from other members of the department the same sort of devotion that he himself was ready to give.[10] The intense conscientiousness with which he managed this added to his troubles and created a strong temptation to accept very generous offers made in the United States. But this too helped to put him in a strong position in intra-departmental bargaining.

Innis was not only an effective head at Toronto; he was the directing spirit of social science in Canada, at least in academic circles. His influence was probably greatest at the University of Saskatchewan where he was represented by his former student and close friend, George Britnell. Mabel Timlin has reported that on her first visit to see Innis after she joined the department in Saskatchewan she was virtually grilled for details on the situation there, and was given the impression that the sort of grilling she got was the usual sort of thing for visitors from the west. Elsewhere, Innis' presence would have been felt more indirectly through his

10 Of those who worked under him, many complained that he seemed to think that academics took vows of hard work, high devotion, and low pay.

position on the Social Science Research Council.[11] He was prominent in the foundation of the Council and took an active interest in
its work by serving on a number of its committees and by being
chairman of the whole Council in 1945–6. His influence, however,
is more evident in the fact that while the chairmanships of all other
committees passed from member to member annually, he remained
chairman of the Grants-in-Aid Committee for the first nine years
of the Council's life. Funds available for research in the social sciences were minuscule by present standards, but almost none of them
was allocated without Innis' knowledge. He met regularly, for hours
on end, with Anne Bezanson, representative of the Carnegie Foundation, to pour over names and projects related to research in social
science in Canada. In the light of all this one would have thought
Innis to have had great influence over the direction of economics in
Canada, and in some sense he did; but one has to remember that
although he criticized severely Keynesian policies, Canada was one
country that positively proclaimed an intention to try them.

By the end of the war Innis was a mature and respected member
of the international academic community, not only as a man of influential position but as a social scientist. He was deeply involved in
the Economic History Association and the American Economic
Association, being at some time president of both. His concern,
however, was never with the merely organizational aspects of those
institutions. A long and earnest correspondence with Arthur H. Cole
in connection with the Committee on Research in Economic History
showed him to be interested only in how those bodies could advance
work on what he considered the most fundamental and pressing
problems of the times. In these last years he felt free to use his position to ask the questions he himself thought important and to muster
resources to answer them. Along with this freedom came the irresistible temptation to let his mild, misanthropic anarchism show
through. What can be said of someone who would give the presidential address to the Royal Society in an old tweed jacket and
baggy trousers, and who would choose as his topic the extent to
which church and state had combined in Canada to keep the common man down? At times his friends tried to talk him out of this

11 This body eventually became part of the Canada Council.

negative frame of mind. They were no more successful in dissuading him than were the scores of influential citizens, private and public, who were forever writing to him to complain about his alleged radical and irresponsible statements. He did have a great sense of humour, nonetheless, and in the end he fell into a witty and bemused sort of pessimism.

The nationalism of the Jews left them without a country. The Roman Catholic Church renounced the world and became the heir of the defunct Roman Empire. Universal suffrage heralded the end of parliamentary government ... The impact of Point Four on other cultures, the clash of so-called 'backward' and so-called 'forward' countries involves such unpaid costs as the enormous loss of life directly through war and indirectly through cultural change ... Each civilization has its own method of suicide.[12]

12 'Industrialism and Cultural Values,' *The Bias of Communication* (1951), 132–41.

2

Innis at Chicago: values and economic growth

It was the aim of Harold Innis to explain the progress of national wealth in the Canadian case. His work, therefore, is interesting for at least two reasons. It is the first, relatively complete, account of the economic aspect of the growth of the Canadian nation, and it is an attempt to raise the general question of economic growth in such a way as to make possible a fresh set of answers. The importance of the second reason cannot be questioned since the point of paramount interest in the entire field of economic studies is economic growth, the causes of the general progress of the wealth of nations.

Analysis of economic progress can be divided into three broad categories: the economics of relative scarcity, the economics of absolute value, and historical economics. Since each of these was incorporated in the work of Adam Smith his *Enquiry into the Causes of the Wealth of Nations* can be taken as a point of departure in discussing them. In that work the three approaches are woven into a loose fabric that gives the impression of being a solid piece of one material but is not, for whenever Smith attempts to connect the different approaches he falls into difficulty. A detailed critique of Smith's work is not necessary here but some discussion of its relevant aspects is.

The economics of relative scarcity is the approach commonly associated with Adam Smith because those who exploited his theories emphasized that part of his work; that is, the Cosmopolitan economists, the free-trade and *laissez-faire* school of the nineteenth century. That school believed the means to an increase in wealth were at hand and needed only to be applied to the task. Indeed, it taught that in the absence of government interference profits, appearing in the form of higher prices, would induce the owners of property to transfer resources into relatively productive employments. Thus price, the measure of relative scarcity, was taken to be the interesting signal in economic growth. As resources were *relatively* scarcified under the direction of the price system, *general* scarcity was presumed to be reduced and economic growth accomplished. The argument was plausible, but failed to explain both the pre-existent surplus to be more efficiently allocated through investment and the conditions under which the relative scarcification of resources would lead to general economic progress.

The weakness of the Cosmopolitan argument was clear to those who felt excluded from the benefits of *laissez-faire*. In particular, Karl Marx attacked the system as a means to economic growth. He thought it was efficient, but that its efficiency depended on the role of coercive property rights, and this had been inadequately represented in the analytical framework founded on the idea of relative scarcity. Marx himself approached the problem more obliquely with a concept of absolute value. Relative value, by definition, could describe only the inter-relations between the various component commodities in an economy. The growth of the entire economy might be related to the structure of these inter-relations, but it might not. Growth, it was conceded by all, was consequent upon the fruitful investment of a surplus over what was necessary to maintain the operation of the economy at any given *level* of wealth and any given *total* size. Therefore, according to Marx, the surplus and its relation to the growth of the economy were subject to analysis only in terms of some idea of absolute value by which the total of commodities could be measured. Unfortunately, however, the Marxian concepts of absolute value and surplus value in their turn failed to explain growth. The idea of surplus is rooted in culture. It is a value judgment and therefore not subject to any merely rational explanation. Like its bourgeois counterpart, the Marxian analysis reduces to a set of theoretical categories in terms of which the growth process can be described without an elaboration of the actual cause and effect relations involved.

Neither the Price economists nor the Marxians came to grips with the basic problem of accumulation, the emergence of a surplus. Smith clearly assumed the existence of a surplus and then proceeded to discuss its efficient allocation.[1] In Marx' view the surplus simply appeared in the system *in an appropriate form* in consequence of the expropriation of labourers by capitalists. This was the aspect of the operation of the bourgeois economic system that he thought to be inadequately represented in the framework of price analysis. Price analysis presumed a primitive distribution of property and then proceeded to a naïve elaboration of a process of exchange in which all were supposed to have reasonably equal bargaining strength. Through exchange an optimal distribution of wealth and rate of growth were supposed to come. At no point was the general level of wage good prices and of wages referred to, thus excluding from discussion the means of effective appropriation of the surplus. Certainly Marx had exposed a fundamental weakness in price economics but he himself had not come to grips with the problem of growth either for he, too, failed to explain the surplus available for expropriation.

In the face of the non-compensating weaknesses of the socialistic approach of Karl Marx and the individualistic approach of the post-Smithian liberals, a third approach, the nationalistic economics of the historians, took shape. The historical economists, like the others, looked to Adam Smith for their beginnings but not to those parts of the *Wealth of Nations* dealing with exchange or accumulation. Rather they took their lead from those parts in which Smith discussed industrial and transportation technique, the habits, customs, and tastes of various peoples, and the effects of different economic systems. From this point they tried to develop theories of economic growth based on concepts of increasing returns to scale of operations, non-continuous advances in industrial technique, the effects of wars and education, available resources and the like. In short,

1 *The Wealth of Nations* (London, 1776; reissued, 1933), Book II, Introduction and c3.

like the Marxians, they centred their attention on the framework of the price system, but, unlike either the Marxians or the price economists, they were not directly concerned with the saving and investment process. They took cognizance in particular of advances in technology, geographical discovery, and aspirational change as inter-related elements in the growth process of socio-economic systems.

The historical school was by no means a homogeneous group of scholars. Some of them despaired of developing a satisfactory theoretical reconstruction of economic progress. Depending on their philosophical options these accepted a pluralistic approach or left the ultimate explanations to chance or to what has been called the human equation, thus introducing the idea of uncertainty at every point in their explanations and precluding the possibility of a closed theoretical reconstruction. Others were not so ready to write off either the price approach or the accumulation approach. They thought there was sufficient degree of determinancy in the social system as a whole to justify a continued effort at developing a theory of economic progress. The German school in particular continued the search for economic theory using the historical approach.

The German school of historical economics was inspired by the notion that while the price approach alone was inadequate it could be made adequate if accompanied by a treatment of the institutional and technological framework of the price system. They then elaborated various stages through which developing economies passed; each stage having its own socio-technological ingredients and peculiar cultural spirit. Even so they did not effectively explain the increase in wealth because they did not explain the process by which societies passed from one stage to another. In the end the historians relied on a *mélange* of factors involving elements gathered from the Marxian approach, from price economics and from the economists of uncertainty, none of whom had an adequate theory.

Towards the end of the nineteenth century all three schools were subjected to severe criticism by Thorstein Veblen who thought them biased by moral considerations incompatible with a scientific approach. In the case of price theory the moral element was embodied in the subjective, hedonistic conception of behaviour typified in the

utilitarian ethics of Jeremy Bentham. Following the lines of thought
dictated by that starting point the neoclassical economists had developed a body of doctrine that pertained entirely to values, that is to
individual normative choice and to the distribution of wealth in con-
formity with the social structure within which individual choice
expressed itself. In no way did the main direction of its elaboration
or its conclusions follow from the concrete, technical characteristics
of the process of production which, in Veblen's view, were the
controlling factors in the progress of wealth. The Marxian economics he considered to be equally impregnated with this hedonistic
approach, though there the hedonism pertained to classes rather
than individuals and was confused with Hegelian idealism through
the use of the concept of dialectics. The confusions of both approaches, so he said, produced an unacceptable turn of argument
that followed the demands of some unquestioned and, in fact, un-
stated norm in the progress of society. In like manner he dismissed
what he called the Historical school for its too close association
with the romantic idealism of mid-nineteenth-century Europe.

Veblen's own theory of the advance of wealth ('civilization')
ran in terms of efficient rather than normative causality. That is to
say, the direction of human effort was explained by objective constraints rather than subjective purpose. On this ground he considered his own to be a scientific and genetic (evolutionary) theory of
economic growth (development). The advance of wealth, so the
theory ran, took place under the motive force of a number of non-
purposive, instinctive human drives such as idle curiosity, workmanship, and the parental bent. These 'blind' or 'opaque' forces were
allegedly directed into specific activity by habit. Habit, in turn, was
structured by successful adaptation to the exigencies of environment. Environment, in its turn, was constituted in consequence of
technique flowing from the exercise of the blind forces of workmanship, curiosity and the like. Clearly this process of interaction was
circular. The story of the advance of civilization, in consequence,
was essentially an account of how creative forces, creative in the
crude sense of technical productivity, had broken free from the
circle. At this point, however, Veblen himself came into difficulty.
Unlike earlier theorists he had no difficulty in explaining the emer-

gence of a surplus to be invested. It was consequent upon costless technological advance. (While this over-simplifies, it brings out clearly his answer to the problem of the earlier doctrines.) Veblen's problem lay in explaining how, precisely, new technology liberated itself from obsolescent institutions in the circular interaction described above. He handled the difficulty by resorting to historical description, thus obfuscating the fact that either the principle of chance or some purposive human action was the only logical resort for an explanation. Of course he could not admit this and still pretend to a scientific theory of the advance of civilization.

It was from this stage to which Veblen had brought the discussion of economic growth, that Harold Innis began his enquiry. One may even anticipate some of the main lines of Innis' work from points that Veblen made. For example, Innis never gave serious consideration to the idea that the saving and investment process should be considered the central point of discussion in a theory of growth. (This, of course, effectively removes his work from the category of modern growth theory which does make the saving and investment process the central point of discussion. It does not, however, classify him with that branch of economics called the theory of economic development. The theory of economic development is distinguishable from the theory of growth precisely in so far as the former deals with the framework of the saving and investment process. Economic development is the economic historian's approach. Innis was concerned directly with the emergence of a surplus to be invested. If he is to be categorized, then he must be placed somewhere between the modern categories of development and growth theory.) Like Veblen, Innis repeatedly insisted that the relatively rapid advance of areas of recent economic growth was a consequence of the application of advanced technology to the virgin resources of areas free from the constraint of obsolescent institutions. There were, however, some points in Veblen's work that Innis did not accept. In particular, he did not accept the proposed scheme of instinctive drives as the motive force of economic advance. In place of that approach, which was crucial to Veblen's idea of scientific economics, Innis seems to have adopted two ideas current at the University of Chicago when he was there.

First was the idea that unity of social purpose does not consist in agreement but in organization. That is to say, social values, the goals of society, are not to be found in expressed agreement but in the rules that direct group behaviour. Second was the idea that new forms of social action do represent values even though these values will at first have no monetary expression. Monetary value will generally reflect the social value embodied in long-established organizations. In other words social values are expressed in the way society organizes around its technical means and only after this organizational framework has been established for some time will prices reflect social values. Clearly, this conceptualization reintroduced the idea of purposive action.

The idea of a meaningfully organized society was close to the organic concept of society of the nineteenth-century German Historical school but it was not idealistic in the Hegelian sense that had been the basis of Veblen's criticism of that group. It did not involve directly the description of a phase in development, rather it provided an explanation of the on-going process of institutional formation, the genetic process of organizational change in relation to changes in technique. Specifically, it was an assertion that as society organized around new techniques, particularly techniques of communication, the purposive character of the general advance received expression in changing institutional forms. These institutional forms constituted a framework within which individual values, expressed in prices, were accommodated. In other words, social values related to the general advance of society were, in theory, logically prior to the market values of the price system; and prices and price theory, though not irrelevant, were somewhat beside the main point in an analysis of economic growth.

However useful these new ideas were to be, by themselves they left the argument about growth theory scarcely advanced beyond the term to which Veblen had carried it. By incorporating a notion of institutional formation in which room was left for free and deliberate human action they provided a more cogent explanation of successive escapes from the constraint of obsolescent institutions. This was all to the good, but the problem of growth theory after Veblen lay in the scientific validity of its conclusions. Veblen strained after a thoroughly scientific theory but in the end based his explanation of growth on chance, and chance is hardly the basis of a scientific theory. The new ideas based the explanation on purposive action rather than chance, which was more plausible; but purposive, free human action is no more a suitable basis for scientific theory than is the principle of chance.

By the time Innis arrived at the University of Chicago the implications of the theoretical dispute were already evident in the content of courses and in the way in which they were being taught. Innis' director, the economic historian, Chester Wright, was working with L.C. Marshall and James Field on an experiment in teaching methods. Their activities led to two new series of publications, 'Materials for the Study of Economics' and 'Materials for the Study of Business,' which were intended to replace the usual sort of theoretical textbook. They were, in fact, an ill-disguised critique of contemporary price theory. As Marshall put it, what was needed was 'not so much authoritative formulations of economic laws as concrete case material embodying such laws.'[2] At first the new 'case and problem presentation of economics' was thought to be suitable as a supplement to textbook economics at intermediate and senior levels only. By 1923 the books were being proposed as substitutes for traditional texts at the beginner's level and criticism of the older texts became explicit. Again as Marshall put it, 'the usefulness in an introductory course of building the presentation about the abstract type of value and distribution ... has been repeatedly questioned by experienced teachers in economics.'[3] In 1925 and 1926 two high-school texts were added to the series, *The Story of Human Progress* and *Readings in the Story of Human Progress*. In these simplified presentations it became very clear that the approach taken was a derivative of the work of Thorstein Veblen.

In teaching one of the experimental courses under Wright's direction Innis became so involved that his own work, in his earliest years, cannot be understood apart from it. The first course he taught at the University of Toronto was a new course in commerce, for

2 L.C. Marshall, C.W. Wright, and J.A. Field, *Materials for the Study of Elementary Economics*, v.
3 L.C. Marshall, *Our Economic Organization* (New York, 1923), v–vi.

the content of which he himself was responsible. In this he drew on his experience at Chicago where L.C. Marshall had conducted the commerce courses. Both the little book of student essays, *The Fur Trade in Canada,* which he edited in 1927, and the first volume of *Select Documents in Canadian Economic History,* which he edited in 1929, were derivatives of the case and problem presentation that had been characteristic of the Chicago experiment. The latter volume was fittingly dedicated to Chester Wright since it was in fact a Canadian volume in the series *Materials for the Study of Elementary Economics.*

Whatever the immediate effects of the dispute on Innis' work, the ultimate resolution of the problem in his own mind was far more important for his understanding of the scientific character of economics and the process of economic advance. In this regard his close contact with Frank Knight, J.M. Clark, and Morris Copeland at Chicago was crucial.

From 1919 through 1922 all three were involved in a series of round table discussions in which they attempted to meet the arguments of R.G. Tugwell and A.B. Wolfe with respect to the scientific character of economics.[4] The points disputed were not specifically points in growth theory, but clearly a resolution of the broader question would have serious implications for the more specific study. The marked influence of this discussion on Innis became most evident when he himself entered it in the late nineteen-twenties and early nineteen-thirties.

Neither Tugwell nor Wolfe believed that a truly scientific economics had been developed or could be developed easily, but both saw an imperative need for it and asserted that it was a possibility. They disagreed with certain aspects of neoclassical thought but wanted to revise it only in so far as its aspirations to a scientific character could be realized. Specifically, they protested against the deductive character of the older theory and proposed that it be replaced by theory based on inductive experiment or statistical investigation, though ultimately their reconstruction implied that

4 The positions taken by these men in the discussions were eventually
   published in a volume of articles, *The Trend of Economics,* from which
   the account here has been drawn.

policy could be deduced from known values. In this sense they were
merely revisionists, however radically different their position was
in any other sense.

In Tugwell's assessment the weaknesses of neoclassical theory
followed upon its attempted deduction of policy from the characteristics of a static model. In reality, he said, there is constant change
and no point of equilibrium is ever reached. Continuous changes
in technology and institutions prevent anything like a normal price
from ever being established. On this ground it seemed clear to him
that scientific economics could not be built with the deductive
methods of the past. It seemed equally evident to him that the
advance of civilization had come to a stage of such complexity that
social science would be necessary to government if it was to govern
well. In fact he seems to have envisioned a group of scientist-
directors implementing a social policy that had been formulated
through statistical induction. To some of those who listened to him
the vision was frighteningly utopian, but not to himself. He admitted
that the new system would require some personal adjustments but
educational institutions with their ability to 'change human nature
from what it is to what it wants to be' could accommodate in this
regard. Clearly he was promoting a scientifically planned society,
rationally constructed in every respect. Even standards of conduct
would be 'instrumental,' that is, they would be judged acceptable
only if they led to 'higher living levels and greater achievement.' Of
course his reasoning was circular. He thought that morality, value
judgements, could be founded upon the methods of inductive
science and, accordingly, he wanted a system of economic welfare
based on objective, scientific ethics rather than on the subjective
valuations presupposed in the neoclassical rationalization of the
price system. His precise point in this regard was more obliquely
made by Wolfe. Wolfe thought of economic systems as the organization of means about ends. Without some agreement about ends
organization would be impossible. Certainly a 'scientifically' constructed system would mean prior agreement on ends. The only
possible basis for this agreement, according to Wolfe, was the
'mechanical' or determined character of human behaviour. Determined behaviour is 'subject to nature's laws' and such laws can be

discovered by empirical science. Like Tugwell, Wolfe was convinced of the need for a scientific social science. Since social science deals with human behaviour either he had to assert the possibility of scientific ethics or, as he himself put it, 'shut up shop.'

In opposition to the optimistic liberal thrust of the revisionist argument Frank Knight appeared sceptical and conservative. His argument centred precisely on the limitations of the scientific method in the analysis of human behaviour, limitations that stemmed, he asserted, from the radical indeterminacy of the subject. This was a firm basis of attack on both the scientism of the revisionists and the presumptions of traditional theory. In regard to the latter Knight said that 'life is at bottom an exploration in the field of values, an attempt to discover values, rather than on the basis of knowledge of them to produce and enjoy them to the greatest extent.'[5] Human behaviour, in his view, was radically indeterminate and creative, whereas science presumes uniformity and predictability. Behaviourist laws were by definition incapable of dealing with the artfulness of humanity, any statistical evidence notwithstanding. The significance of statistical uniformity in actions was in part based on a presumption of independent action by individuals. But people copy the artful actions of others and a radically free decision becomes an epidemic of similar decisions. For Knight the inductive approach was no more adequate than the deductive approach and for the same reasons. Even Veblen's earlier attempt to construct an inductive social science was as abstracted from the content of human action as price theory. Tugwell had claimed that such a science was becoming increasingly necessary as society advanced into greater complexity. Knight took the opposite view. The more advanced society becomes the farther man gets from the elemental factors in life and the more artificial he and his organizations become, and consequently, the less predictable human behaviour becomes. At every point, then, he opposed the idea of scientific ethics and scientific social science.

The implication of Knight's assertions for the development of the

5 This seems to be the basic psychological or moral tenet underlying Knight's work in *Risk, Uncertainty and Profit* (Boston, 1921) and in his later writings on the place of ethics in economics.

theory of economic progress are evident. The theory would have to accommodate the indeterminate artfulness of human choice, and values would have to be regarded as one of the independent and essential roots of growth. Helpful as the price theory approach or the statistical approach might be, the ethical or value approach was also necessary. This point was clearly grasped by Innis, and his contribution to growth or development theory followed upon his attempt to reduce to a minimum the intractable problem of values. Veblen's work was too appealing for Innis to give up entirely the idea that a scientific approach was necessary, but Knight's scepticism and open mindedness was an opposite pole of attraction. If Innis did not accept Veblen's hypothesis regarding non-purposive, instinctive behaviour as the engine of economic change it was probably because this was the point in the Veblenian system at which Knight's attack was directed. The result was a hiatus in the logical structure of Innis' perception of the growth process. Because of this hiatus his own thinking developed on independent lines.

Innis accepted the idea of social values developing pragmatically and insinuating themselves gradually into the price system through institutional change, as outlined earlier, and modified it with Knight's notion that values are creative, artful, radically free and indeterminate. The result was a basic concept of the role of institutional formation in the process of economic advance, that is, that the function of institutional formation is to liberate social action to accommodate new circumstances and new goals (values), particularly to permit the realization of new possibilities that do not receive expression in the price valuation of established markets. It was a simple but problematic point of departure for building a theory of the progress of wealth because the theory built upon it could approximate a scientific character only to the extent that the role of values was limited. But to raise this dilemma is to get too far ahead in the development of Innis' thinking. He had much economic history and theory to work through before he himself made it explicit.

There were other aspects of Knight's work that made a lasting impression on Innis. As the debate of the nineteen-twenties continued into the next decade positions shifted, but in one way or another they continued to focus on the value element in the functioning of social systems. In 1932, in a review of Sumner Slichter's *Modern Economic Society*,[6] Knight restated his previous arguments against the extreme revisionist position, making side references to R.G. Tugwell who, with Slichter, he categorized as 'another leader of the Newer Economics.' In this instance, however, Knight added a lengthy analysis of the process by which the 'Newer Economics' was coming to be accepted as 'truth.' The review was an essay on the sociology of talk or, more specifically, on 'discussion in the social sciences.' In essence it was a statement of the limitations of social science in forming the sort of intelligence required for a directed society and of the limitations of intelligence, however formed, in the direction of society. Combined as it was with suggestions on how the very limited social science that existed was in fact being institutionalized into government, it was anything but an optimistic statement. On the other side, the optimism of the revisionists seemed to be boundless. In 1934 Tugwell reasserted his faith in a 'managed society' and in 'the real possibility that society may become a function of education.'[7] Knight responded with an analysis of the nationalistic bias in economic theory,[8] which he presented to the economic history discussion group at the meetings of the American Economic Association. When Innis, who chaired the discussion, reported it in the papers and proceedings of the Association he mentioned only A.B. Wolfe as having disagreed with the main speaker. By that time, however, Innis himself was personally caught up in the debate and was spinning off articles on the question.[9]

J.M. Clark's contribution to the discussions of the early nineteen-twenties was as value oriented as the others, but he carried his argument farther beyond the point of mere criticism of traditional theory. Like the rest of the participants he was not explicitly inter-

6 F.H. Knight, 'The Newer Economics and the Control of Economic Activity.'
7 R. Tugwell, *Redirecting Education* (New York, 1934).
8 This paper was published as 'Economic Theory and Nationalism' in Knight's *Ethics of Competition*.
9 H.A. Innis, 'Economic Nationalism,' (1934); 'Economics for Demos,' (1934); 'The Role of Intelligence: Some Further Notes,' (1935); 'Discussion in the Social Sciences,' (1936).

ested in growth or development economics, but again the questions of that particular branch of economics insinuated themselves into what he said. Specifically, he attempted to rebuild economics on what he called 'non-Euclidian' propositions drawn from the work of Veblen. 'Machines impose conditions as well as provide services' and one of these conditions is that 'overhead costs are universal.' Another is that habits and institutions adapt to the technical demands of production and consumption. What he was asserting was that price economics, since it reduced the significance of everything to price valuation, was incapable of distinguishing the characteristics of a modern capitalistic economy operating under the technical constraints of the machine industry, and that a new set of concepts was necessary to describe the consequences of the latter condition.[10]

The non-Euclidian economics proved to be most useful to Innis in his description of economic advance in Canada. The boom and collapse sequence characteristic of the development of frontier areas in the railroad era were well typified by Clark's accelerator principle. When Innis used the idea intensively in his studies of the Canadian case, however, he did not cite the 'accelerator principle.' He simply referred to exceedingly rapid economic advance consequent upon the application of advanced techniques to virgin resources.[11] The companion concept of overhead costs, which is only another way of viewing the effects of using advanced technique in building a capitalistic economy, was particularly useful to Innis in his elaboration of the effects of excess capacity in communications and transportation systems.[12]

The years at Chicago evidently provided Innis with questions and approaches that were to preoccupy him for the rest of his life.

10 See his *Studies in the Economics of Overhead Costs* and his seminal article 'Business Acceleration: a Technical Factor in Economic Cycles,' *Journal of Political Economy* 25 (1917), 217–35.
11 Recent textbook presentations (e.g., P.A. Samuelson and A. Scott, *Economics* (Toronto, 1971), 313–7) of the accelerator principle refer almost exclusively to its operation in the capitalistic producer's goods sectors of highly developed economies. Clark was interested in all goods produced in the earlier stages of production and particularly in the raw materials of underdeveloped areas.
12 See his 'The Penetrative Powers of the Price System,' (1938).

On returning to Canada he became involved in the building of Canadian economics and, therefore, had to adapt what he had learned to a study of the frontier in the advance of machine, chemical, and electronic industry. But the problem of the frontier is the problem of growth; and the problem of the economist of the frontier is to explain growth with as much scientific validity as possible. The degree of scientific validity, as the matter had been given to Innis, depended radically on a solution to the problem of values in economic theory. What one is to look for in Innis' work, therefore, is a new answer to the question of economic growth issuing from an examination of the role of values in a frontier economy.

3

The historical case:
Canada

In building the course in Canadian economic history in the previous academic year I had decided that maps were of crucial importance if the general character of Canada was to be understood. In working on my thesis I had gradually come to realize that the Canadian Pacific Railway had linked up a land unit which was basically dependent at an earlier stage on water navigation. It was important therefore to have maps which would show the rivers interlocked from Eastern Canada to the Pacific coast and to restore the idea of unity which had been destroyed by maps relating chiefly to the railroad ...

After the publication of my thesis I was compelled to think out my next fruitful line of study ... I had a further uneasy feeling that my thesis was inadequate and indeed one or two reviews had pointed out this fact. I must therefore satisfy an uneasy conscience by continuing along lines which would offset its defects. I had been greatly influenced by Professor C.S. Duncan in his lectures on marketing by the emphasis on the relationship between the physical characteristics of a commodity and the marketing structure built in relation to it. I had also read intensively as a result of my contact with graduate students in Chicago the [works] of Thorstein Veblen, in which the same point had been made but in a more general fashion ...

I had further to acquire familiarity with the work which had been done in Canada, limited though it was in quality, and to learn something of the archives in Ottawa and elsewhere. The documents in the various archives were of course chiefly concerned with political activities and were much less satisfactory in describing the economic and social conditions of different periods ... I also enlisted the interest of students in the commerce course in the general problems and for four or five years each student in the senior year did an extended essay on some phase of the staple industries of Canada. In these various ways I began to acquire a familiarity with the history of Canada as well as with conditions at the present time. My immediate task was offsetting the limitations of my thesis by attempting to show the inherent unity of Canada as it developed before the railroad in relation to lakes and rivers. For this reason I concentrated in the beginning on the history of the fur trade as the oldest staple trade of the continent.[1]

Clearly neither a theory of growth nor of economic development was evident in Innis' work at the beginning. Most of his earliest efforts during that period of unsteady prosperity prior to the crash of 1929 were directed to historical investigation. Together with factual research, however, he attempted an assessment of the work done by others and this required an analytic framework on his part, bringing him into contact with contemporary attempts to elaborate a theory of economic progress. Thus there were three main aspects of Innis' work, each being a necessary preliminary to its final issue in later years. One element of that issue, however, his judgment in regard to the role of values, remained implicit. It began to form in the late 'twenties but did not clearly assert itself until the depression had thrown both the economy and the economists into confusion. The war came before he attempted explicitly to integrate the value component into his theory of the general progress of wealth.

The analytic framework was Veblen's, or rather, what Innis saw in Veblen and chose to use,[2] a conceptualization built on 'the [presumed] existence of laws of growth and decay of institutions' and designed precisely for 'the study of processes of growth and

1 Innis, 'Autobiography,' 107–8.
2 What Innis distilled from Veblen is clearly stated in Innis' 'A Bibliography of Thorstein Veblen' (1929).

decay.' He judged that no other instrument could be adequate for the analysis of economies accumulating a surplus in the form of modern industrial equipment. The success of Veblen's 'direct and devastating attack on the marginal utility theory' turned Innis away from all but a partial and nominal use of the tools of traditional price economics. In fact he regarded that style of economics as a positive hindrance to understanding the dynamics of growth in the frontier areas of well-developed industrial societies.

Veblen has waged a constructive warfare of emancipation against the standardized static economics which has become so dangerous on a continent with ever increasing numbers of students clamouring for textbooks on final economic theory. He attempted to outline the economics of dynamic change and to work out a theory not only of dynamics but of cyclonics ...

The conflict between the economics of a long and highly industrialized country such as England and the economics of recently new and borrowing countries will become less severe as the theory of cyclonics is worked out.[3]

At this embryonic stage in its development Innis' theory of cyclonics distinguished the growth process of a marginal economy by its relatively rapid pace of advance and by its reversal of the stages of development observed in older areas.[4] Both distinctions were a consequence of the fact that a new country of the satellite variety comes under the influence of the price system and industrialism when the latter have already attained an advanced stage in their formation. The satellite, therefore, receives the last form of things first. When there are improvements in the industrial technique of a developed economy two adjustments of consequence to frontier areas take place. First, to some extent the institutional framework of the price system accommodates itself and, second, following improved technical and economical efficiency the geographical area coming under the influence of the economy expands. Penetration of

3 *Ibid.*, 26.
4 The following is a paraphrase of Innis' 'Industrialism and Settlement in Western Canada' (1930).

new areas is achieved by means of the improved technology, and organization in the areas penetrated is characterized by the appropriate new institutional forms. Now, in the Veblen-Innis scheme this whole process of advance is clearly predicated on prior technological change and, therefore, takes on the characteristics of technological change. The latter, since it depends on improvements in science and engineering, changes progressively and in a cumulative fashion as knowledge builds on and reinforces itself. Thus technological change takes place at an ever increasing pace of advance, bringing with it institutional change, that is, new forms of the price system. Similarly, economic advance in marginal areas takes place at an ever increasing pace until, at an advanced stage of modern industrialism, an entire satellite economy with all its technical and organizational equipment is built in one brief moment of social excitation that can only be described as an economic storm of cyclonic intensity.

The rapid growth of the Canadian economy after 1867 was a clear case in point. Industrialism and the price system had expanded from western Europe to encompass the United States. From there, by a process of 'wholesale borrowing,' they swept northward into Canada. Not only the rapidity of the advance, but also the satellite character of the Canadian economy, its structure, and its dominant type of activity, were dictated by the stage of development in Britain and the United States. The mass production techniques of mechanized, integrated economies require the mass production of raw materials. Consequently the Canadian economy was biased in favour of large-scale production of primary commodities required for the continued advance of mechanized industry in older areas. That is to say, the predominance of staple exports was a consequence of the characteristics of mechanized production. Geographical limitations were important in this regard, but geography takes on importance only in relation to technology. The production of staples was dictated by the technical characteristics of the machine industry primarily, and only secondarily by resource endowment and the process of commodity specialization in the price system.

Innis was only one of several economists working towards a

theoretical framework on which the facts of Canadian history could be hung. All were converging on what has since been called the staples thesis of Canadian economic development, but there were essential differences growing out of their basically dissimilar approaches to the process of economic advance.[5] James Mavor, head of the department of political economy at Toronto when Innis arrived, was the first to try. Mavor had been strongly influenced by the German Historical school and in consequence constructed Canadian history into ill-defined stages of advance. C.R. Fay, a colleague of Innis in the nineteen-twenties, improved on Mavor by defining the stages in terms of successive staple exports. Following the British tradition in economics, Fay drew heavily on the historical analysis presented by Adam Smith, stressing the importance of the means of transportation in economic expansion and commodity specialization between developed and satellite economies. A third important contribution came from another colleague of Innis, G.E. Jackson. Jackson was interested in the statistical analysis of business cycles, particularly as that method of study was developed in Britain and the United States. He clearly pointed to the importance of fluctuations in staple exports, specifically wheat, among the factors causing expansion and contraction of the Canadian economy. Of course this was a theory of cycles rather than of development, but the two are related. Finally, W.A. Mackintosh of Queen's University, taking his lead from the frontier thesis of the geographical historian F.J. Turner, used ideas of resource endowment and commodity specialization to adumbrate what has since been generally accepted as the staples thesis.

None of these explanations was acceptable to Innis because none of the approaches used had been designed specifically to deal with the frontier experience. Either they were wanting on the general grounds pointed out by Veblen, as in the case of Mavor's approach, or, being constructed in view of the development processes of British and American industrialism, they were unsuited to the Canadian case. Turner's frontier thesis was close to the point, but it was essentially a theory of the effects of geography, explaining limi-

5 For a review of this work see Innis, 'The Teaching of Economic History in Canada' (1929).

tations on the advance of industrialism but not the advance itself. This weakness in Turner's theory was clearly pointed up by the metropolitan thesis of N.S.B. Gras who asked the pointed question, 'frontier of what?' Unfortunately Gras then answered it by using theories developed in relation to the growth processes of metropolitan areas in Europe. Innis' theory of cyclonics put both approaches together, amended their weaknesses and incorporated a time factor. The only one whose work Innis did not reject was C.R. Fay, but Fay himself later admitted that Innis was doing something different and new.

While the theory of cyclonics was intended as a continuation of the constructive aspects of Veblen's work, it was built on the ruins left by his destructive critique of established styles of economic analysis. The consistent critical stance of Innis' numerous book reviews indicate that he had taken Veblen as the final word on all previous doctrine. Whenever he thought it was appropriate, he repeated Veblenian ideas such as, 'the lack of an impersonal, scientific and objective approach renders the conclusions of a speculative character,' or 'typical of the historical school, but ... nonetheless unscientific.'[6] Works that he praised for their scientific approach were usually geographic interpretations of history but even these he found wanting on the grounds that geography takes on explanatory importance only in relation to technology. In regard to price economics there is the following:

The definition of economics as a science that deals with human interest from the standpoint of price is as questionable as it is unnecessary ... How is it possible ... to present a very sane discussion of 'normal conditions' and then write a meaningless statement to the effect that human beings everywhere and in the long run, except where price fluctuations and unemployment prevent, adjust their efforts as producers to the maximum possibilities of their pleasures as consumers? What is meant when it is said that the right prices are those which stimulate a country to its maximum continuous output ... maximum production consistent with human satisfaction? The shades of hedonism stalk through a

6 Innis, review of *Land Settlement in Upper Canada, 1783–1840* by G.C. Paterson (1923).

treatise on money ... It is hoped further that a time will arrive when it will not be possible to label a paragraph, 'capital goods are the result of saving.'[7]

In regard to the statistical approach we have evidence of his very Veblenian attitude to the importation of economic styles developed in older countries.

The situation was inevitably the result of the wholesale borrowing of statistical apparatus by a new country from older countries. The dangers are serious. The faith shown in recently established organizations such as the Tariff Board, the increasing attention to mathematical acrobatics in the subject of money and price statistics, the rise and fall of forecasting services ... all the result of the belief in the certainty of statistics. These evils are associated with the confusion, characteristic of new countries, of statistics with economics.[8]

But these merely suggestive citations are not drawn from an important part of his writings. Apparently he considered Veblen's work quite adequate in this regard and he passed on to the task of building up a theory of growth suitable to the Canadian case.

We come then to Innis' own contribution to Canadian economics as it grew out of his still embryonic concept of cyclonics. That concept itself continued to develop, of course, and this affected the character of the more historical works which will be discussed in this chapter. Every effort will be made to make that explicit and clear, though a fuller exposition of the cyclonic process as it appears in its most developed form will be left for the next chapter. How Innis used it to analyse the contemporary situation in Canada, and how this in turn forced him to face squarely the problematic role of values, will be dealt with in the chapter after that.

The dissertation, *A History of the Canadian Pacific Railway* (1923), was begun before the idea of cyclonics emerged at all, but its revision for publication was carried out during the period in which Innis was reading Veblen. The result was a peculiar dicho-

7 Innis, review of *Money* by W.T. Foster and W. Catchings (1923).
8 Innis, review of *The Canada Year Book* (1929).

tomy between the empirical work in the body of the study and the theorizing of its introduction and conclusion. The latter were written last and clearly marked by Veblen's influence. As reviews pointed out, Innis seemed to be imposing on his research a significance that it did not have. He himself was aware of the problem but there was no help for it because even in later years his conceptual framework continued to evolve ahead of his research. In fact, the whole idea of writing the economic history of Canada in terms of staple products, growing as it did out of the shortcomings of the dissertation, has to be regarded as not typical of the Innisian approach because it was conceived in some sense without direct reference to his mature theoretical explanation of economic growth. Having said all this, however, there are little grounds left for further discussion of the *History of the Canadian Pacific Railway*. Its bulk was made up of a mass of factual data centring on problems of finance, debt structure, overhead costs and speed of expansion – a dull but fruitful application of some new concepts to an important aspect of Canadian economic history.

There were three major staples histories, *The Fur Trade in Canada* (1930), *Settlement and the Mining Frontier* (1936), and *The Cod Fisheries* (1940). Each in its turn was marked by an increasingly mature stage in the development of the idea of cyclonics, and each in consequence was more complex in what it tried to say. Being smaller, and more limited in scope, the mining study gives the appearance of being the least affected in this way. *The Cod Fisheries* was sufficiently complex to defy Innis' attempt to put it on paper and to puzzle the most astute of its reviewers. A fourth staple history centring on pulp and paper was begun in the late nineteen-thirties, but the elaboration of cyclonic theory moved into a new and more intense phase at that time, finally distracting Innis from the staples-as-case-study approach. This history was never completed. Sometime between the first and second histories he shifted his attention from staple products as such to staples in relation to means of transportation. This brought his approach more into line with the idea of cyclonics by putting greater emphasis on the effects of technological advance at the metropolitan centre of expansion. Clear evidence of the shift can be found in the different organization of material in the two volumes of historical documents which he edited in the period.[9] The first volume was organized largely on chronological lines but showed a strong tendency to centre attention on the characteristics of commodities, reflecting the general staples approach of contemporary Canadian economic history, and particularly the approach of C.R. Fay. In the second volume the emphasis was entirely upon the characteristics of means of transportation. After 1930 it was Fay, not Innis, who wrote the history of the empire by commodities.[10] The later phase of Innis' interest in transportation, commencing in 1940, involved a widening of attention to include all media of communication and their implications for the value component in economic advance. It was this final step in the maturation of the idea of cyclonics that distracted him completely from the fourth staples history.

Notwithstanding its clear lines of evolution, there is a point of view from which it can be seen that all of Innis' work was of one piece. In 1929 the first volume of the *Select Documents* began with a general statement of interest.

The spread of western civilization in North America has been largely determined in its nature and extent by the character and number of the population, by the institutional equipment of the European settlers, by the advancement of the industrial arts known to them, by the cultural background of the native peoples of North America and also by such inter-related geographic circumstances as climatic conditions, geological formations, topographical features, and flora and fauna.[11]

In 1944, when the continuity of his thought was no longer apparent even to those who were closely associated with him, he again made a general statement of interest.

The effects of geography may be offset by technology ... Geography

---

9 Innis (ed.), *Select Documents in Canadian Economic History* vol. 1 (1929), vol. 2 (1933).
10 Further evidence of the shift in Innis' approach can be found in his articles, 'Transportation as a Factor in Canadian Economic History' (1931), and 'Unused Capacity as a Factor in Canadian Economic History' (1936).
11 *Select Documents in Canadian Economic History: 1479–1873,* vol. 1 (1929), xxix.

provides the grooves which determine the course and to a large extent the character of economic life. Population in terms of numbers and quality, and technology are largely determined by geographic background, and political institutions have been to an important extent shaped through wars in relation to this background.[12]

The major difference between the two statements is a trivial reversal of the order in which the points of interest are mentioned. We have here, therefore, directives for discovering what Innis was saying in the staples histories.

The Fur Trade in Canada (1930) is a meticulous study of the forces working in favour of the formation of Canada as a distinct, unified, political entity.[13] Throughout the volume attention is focused on forms of commercial enterprise as the main factor in political organization. Particular emphasis is placed on the process of organizational growth, turning the history of the fur trade into an account of the struggle between competitive and monopolistic forms of enterprise. During the French period heavy social overhead in the form of military facilities for defence against the British led to extreme centralization of economic activities. Following the conquest this overhead was unnecessary, and a more decentralized, competitive organization of traders moved north from the New England colonies. The new organization increased the efficiency with which furs were taken, but for this very reason it was the occasion of a rapid exhaustion of the fur-bearing animals and of an increased uncertainty in regard to profits. Exhaustion of fur supplies necessitated further penetration into the hinterland, raising overhead costs because of longer supply lines and a slower turnover of goods. Gradually competition gave way to amalgamation for the sake of centralized handling of supplies, concentration of capital to meet heavier fixed costs, and the reduction of uncertainty. In 1821 monopoly was again established with the union of the North West Company and the Hudson's Bay Company.

The demands of the trade were reflected in the organization of

12 Innis, 'On the Economic Significance of Culture' (1944).
13 I have not given page references for the following points since there is hardly a page from 9 through 379 on which one or more of them is not either made or documented.

enterprise, and those of enterprise in that of politics. In the beginning the staple export was an economic inducement to the centre of
expansion in Europe and a reason for the continued existence of the
colony within a mature price system. Other economic and political
activities in the colony were either a support for the staple trade
or a consequence of its alternating successes and failures. Thus the
success of the British in holding territory seized from the French
followed upon their success in the trade. Success in the trade, in
turn, depended upon the superiority of British over French industry,
from the point of view of cheaper commodities to exchange for
furs, and upon the superiority of the British in transportation, both
from the point of view of technique and adaptability inland and
from the point of view of naval control on the ocean. At the same
time continuity in the economic function and political organization
of the colony as it passed from French to English control indicated
the general similarity between the French and English economies.
The relatively underdeveloped condition of the United States' industry immediately after 1776 would have necessitated a severe adjustment of economic and political organization had the northern
colonies decided to join the revolutionaries. In short, existing enterprise and its concomitant political organization were highly resistant
to a severance of the British connection.

As Fay pointed out, the conclusion to the history of the fur trade
was not a comment on the early period of Canadian development.
It was a comment on twentieth-century Canada made in the light of
the history of the fur trade and it was a further attempt to build
up the theory of cyclonics. The conclusion began where the history
of the fur trade ended. By 1820 continued industrial advance at the
centre of expansion and exhaustion of supplies of fur led to the
emergence of timber as the dominant staple export. Demand for
timber was connected with the use of the steam engine in Britain
while canals and improvements in transportation connected with the
steam engine facilitated exploitation of Canadian supplies. On the
one hand, heavy initial capital expenditures on the new transportation system reinforced the centralized structure of the economy.
On the other, the existence of centralization made it possible to
accommodate the new phase of industrialism in fairly short order.

The large measure of continuity that marked this and subsequent adjustments were evident in the transfer of both personnel and organization from the Hudson's Bay Company through the Grand Trunk Railway to the government of Canada and the Canadian Pacific Railway. Clearly the interaction of the demands of the machine industry and the kind of organization it engendered biased the economy towards a particular type and pace of economic growth. After 1896 the pattern was repeated as settlement and wheat production in western Canada and industrialization in central Canada were established in the process of an economic cyclone that left in its wake the problems of twentieth-century Canada. In sum, the existence, extent and character of the Canadian nation had been the natural consequence of a continuous interaction of geography, technology, and institutions, extending back to the beginning of the fur trade and building up in cumulative reinforcement into the present.

The other two staple histories, *The Cod Fisheries* (1940) and *Settlement and the Mining Frontier* (1936), differed from the first not only in their basic conceptual framework but also in their historical intent. *The Fur Trade* substantiated a theme of Canadian unity and continuity over time, whereas the others explored the diversity of Canada and its uneven development through different phases of industrial advance. To say that Innis revised Canadian history to show that the nation was not built in defiance of geography and economics is entirely misleading. He exposed the underlying forces both of unity and diversity, for the most part emphasizing the latter. There were periods in which unifying forces predominated, that is, when fur and wheat were the dominant staples; but with fish, timber, minerals, and pulp and paper this was not the case. Alternatively, and more properly from the Innisian point of view, river transportation and railways produced centralization and unity whereas the sailing ship, canals, and the automobile produced decentralization and disunity.

Research for *The Cod Fisheries*, providing as it did an opportunity to examine both the rise and the decline of an economic system, was a more fruitful exercise from the point of view of Innis' search for the laws of growth and decay. As the story of the fur trade centred on persistent pressures in the direction of centralization, so the story of the Maritimes centred on a change from decentralization to centralization and the decline of institutions shaped by the former tendency. Where the history of the fur trade had been marked by a contest between monopolistic and competitive forms of business enterprise, the history of the cod fisheries was marked by a similar but more profound conflict. A decentralized economic system came to a degree of maturity only to be eroded and rendered obsolescent by the incursions and competition of a centralized economic system.

Innis told the story from the point of view of the rise and internal problems of the decentralized system. Its existence began when, through improved maritime transportation, easily exploited fishing grounds were opened up to Europe. The capital commitment in the fisheries as such was negligible and the investment in shipping was economically and physically mobile. Not that shore installations were unimportant, for bases of supply in the area of operations added to efficiency and eventually liberated the coastal trade in North America from dependence on Europe, concomitantly liberating it from the mercantilistic controls necessary for coping with the uncertainties and longer time horizons of the trans-Atlantic trade. The economic system that emerged on the basis of coastal shipping was, in Innis' terminology, commercial. That is, it was characterized by minimal capitalization, easy entry, consequent decentralization, and, within its own framework, flexibility in the face of shifting opportunities for profit. All the basic lines of organization and economic efficiency in the system militated against the tight political controls of European economic imperialism. Thus, when Spain and France competed with England for dominance in the north-west Atlantic, English superiority in the coastal trade was the basis of long-run victory. Eventually, however, the English themselves were defeated by the forces that had defeated the Spanish and the French, for the problems of centralized political control re-emerged prior to the American revolution. The significant victory was not the victory of one nation over another but of commercialism over mercantilism. Shifts in national dominance were symptoms of political problems caused by the bias towards decentralization in the maritime economic system.

The main turning point and central fact in the whole story was the eventual defeat of the commercial system itself. With the advent of steam transportation and the demands it made in terms of heavy capitalization, centralization, and the development of new products, the commercialism of the maritime economy became technologically and institutionally obsolescent. Its final collapse, however, was preceded by a brief period of economic and political flowering as the conflicting tendencies of the transition momentarily supported one another. The Bluenose schooner became the pride of the sea and Nova Scotia became the first colony in British North America to achieve political independence and responsible government. In the most extreme case, however, that of Newfoundland, complete decentralization of political power during the commercial period left the island helpless in the face of change. In Nova Scotia some possibility of inland development and an advantageous position for organized bargaining within the British Empire created a counteraction of centripetal and centrifugal forces that expressed itself politically in the emergence of representative government. This development, in turn, according to Innis, through the influence of ideas and men, affected the structure of confederation in Canada as a whole, mitigating the centralizing bias of areas developing rapidly in relation to railway transportation. After 1885 further penetration of the Maritimes by enterprise based in central Canada and the United States undermined the commercial system and left it the economic and political captive of continental industrialism.

Taking the work as a whole, the significant thing about *The Cod Fisheries* is its clarification of focus. It is not about cod, but is rather an analysis of the shifting structure of a politico-economic system in relation to technical changes affecting primarily the dominant means of transportation. From there it was a short step to Innis' later work on empire and communications.

The last staple history, *Settlement and the Mining Frontier*, was a relatively short monograph lacking the broad historical intent of the other two. It was, nonetheless, the expression of an important aspect of Innis' thinking in regard to both Canadian history and the theory of cyclonics. In it he touched on the most recent phase of Canada's economic development, the era of electricity, automobiles, newsprint and light metals, and on the concomitant divisive impact of American continental industrialism in Canada. From the point of view of cyclonic theory the study was an explicit advance since, in his portrayal of the Klondike gold rush as an ideal type of cyclonic development, Innis clarified his idea of the role of finance in economic advance. All of that we leave to be elaborated in the next chapter.

In all three staple histories there was much that clearly indicated Innis' search for economic theory, but little to indicate that the main line of his progress was approaching the problematic role of values. This was evident only in the questions that he did not ask and the logical steps he did not take. At every point in the histories he left a place for values as one of the determinants of institutional forms. As he himself said, 'a history of trade and commerce ... is essentially a history of associations that permit growth.'[14] In other words the character of institutional formation in the growth process is essentially creative and policy-oriented. Through institutional formation, values are embodied in the structure of economic activity, and therefore an explanation of economic advance is impossible unless the determinants of values can be specified. The force of this point came home to Innis at the beginning of the depression, but again, before that can be properly recounted, it will be necessary to outline the theory of cyclonics and to show how it was used in analysis of the Canadian economy.

14 Innis, review of *A History of Trade and Commerce with Special Reference to Canada* by H. Heaton (1928).

4

The theory of
economic growth

Innis' concern with questions pertaining immediately to the theory of economic growth, as that term is commonly understood, was most intense between 1928 and 1935. Even in that period, however, he did not explicitly elaborate a theory of growth, and his partial and implicit theorizing was unorthodox.[1] It was unorthodox from any point of view and so neither can it be fitted neatly into the categories of the theory of development. Growth theory centres on the saving and investing processes in accumulation, approaching the subject from the point of view of the limitations set by available surplus and diminishing returns. Development theory centres on the character of resources, technology, institutions and values, and the effects of innovation in these areas over time. Innis used both approaches, but only as they had a bearing on the advance of marginal or satellite economy. Following the demands of his interest, he spent his time exploring the possibilities of both types of theory, testing their uses in a number of directions and pushing forward the frontier of knowledge.

If the nature of Innis' contribution is to be understood, an

1 As W.A. Mackintosh and Ken Buckley suggest. See Mackintosh's 'Innis on Canadian Economic Development,' *Journal of Political Economy*, 61 (1935), 185–94; and Buckley's 'The Role of Staple Industries in Canadian Economic Development,' *Journal of Economic History*, 28 (1958), 439–52.

attempt will have to be made to reconstruct the partially implicit foundations of his growth-and-development theory. In some measure the exercise will be hypothetical, but only up to that point in the logical elaboration of the theory at which it is possible to cite Innis' explicit statements. From that point on the theory is what he said it was. We come then at last to a constructive interpretation of the Innisian theory of economic progress, a formulation of what he called cyclonics.

The *price system,* as Innis used the term, is an organizational structure that is accidental, not necessary, to economic activity. Economic activity as such is merely the production, distribution and consumption of goods and services. When this is organized according to the price system the specifying elements are private property, the use of money as a medium of exchange, and the acceptance of rates of exchange set by free market forces. Thus, under the institutional constraints of the price system, economic activity is an inter-related set of exchanges in which all parties benefit, because each has a surplus of the goods given in relation to the goods received or the exchange does not take place. Within the system the medium of exchange provides a common measure of value – because money price under ideal conditions is an index of the market's consensus as to the benefit to be derived from one good in relation to that to be derived from others. That is to say, market prices are a means of communicating throughout the system a consensus as to the relative value of any commodity or service. Now the advantage of this communication lies in the fact that with it exchange can take place in abstraction from the subjective, relative valuation attached to goods by individuals. The use of the money measure, in other words, provides an index of relative scarcities in the whole set of inter-related exchanges on the basis of which *commerce,* buying and selling as a socio-economic function separate from production and consumption, comes into existence. The price system is, at least, a commercial system.

In a price system money is part of the framework of economic activity, even though it appears to enter into exchange as does any other commodity. Its operations approximate those of a commodity but there are special differences. For the present purposes the important specific difference lies in the fact that money, whether book credit or 'hard cash,' is immediately acceptable in exchange throughout the system. Goods may not be. Thus the possession of money, however obtained, carries with it a command over goods and services. More to the point, money is the most *liquid* item of exchange precisely because it can readily be transformed into other items, whereas other items may not be readily transformed.

Exchange takes place in *space* and *time*. A price system, therefore, will have a spatial and temporal dimension. The spatial dimension relates to geographic area and population size. Spatial limits in any case are defined as the boundaries within which exchange of any commodity in question will take place, that is by the existence of a common market. Now, any economic agent or group of agents will be included in a given market if the money cost of spatial movement of the commodity in question is not so much as to raise its selling price to a point where it would be less expensive for the recipient in the exchange to produce the commodity for himself. In short, the extent of the market will be a function of the money cost of transportation. The money cost of transportation, in turn, will be a function of the relative scarcity of the resources required by the operative technique of communication. With this introduction of the idea of technical means, however, capital (surplus), comes to the fore as an element in the price system and the temporal dimension takes on significance.

The temporal dimension of the price system relates to the length of time elapsing in the process of exchange and therefore is measured by the extent to which payment is foregone or, in other words, by the size of the available surplus of consumer's goods in that period. A commercial system with a short time dimension has a rapid turnover of trade from money to goods to money. A long time dimension implies a slow turnover. In this context, therefore, the commercial transformation of money to goods to money over time is hardly distinguishable from the 'round about method of production.' It might even be better to adopt the terminology of capital (growth) theory and speak of the system of exchanges as having breadth and depth. Lengthening the time dimension would be the same thing as capital deepening. The terminological change, however, would introduce a bias in favour of the mathematical as opposed to the historical concept of time and so would eliminate a significantly distinctive element of the Innisian scheme. But to return to the discussion, in the usual case the introduction of more sophisticated technique will lengthen the time dimension of the system, thus introducing elements of uncertainty into its operations. With a longer time dimension (time horizon), complications arise from the possibility that the consensus of value attached to commodities will change during the process of exchange, that is between the time that the entrepreneur commits himself to the expected price structure and the time at which he realizes the value of his transactions. This uncertainty may lead to windfall losses or gains because longer time horizons introduce effective rigidities into the structure of prices.

Now, while the owner of resources will exchange goods for money for goods, in that order, the entrepreneur, deriving his livelihood by specializing in the operations of the system of exchanges itself, will generally be involved in an exchange of money for goods for money, in that order. If the entrepreneur has not a stock of money of his own at the outset of his operations he will have to establish his credit with someone who has. Credit may be established with a third party or it may be extended by whoever is initially selling goods to the entrepreneur. In any case, credit performs the function of money, in effect is money, but it is not pure liquidity because its character corresponds to the character of the exchange involved. The time horizon of the deal struck requires a corresponding term of credit. Again, long-term credit, implying a certain available surplus or depth of capital, will involve price rigidities over time and uncertainty as to the possibility of transactions.

In accord with his position in the structure of exchanges, an entrepreneur will initiate a deal only if the cost of goods to him is sufficiently lower than the price at which he expects to sell them. Of course, what he thinks sufficient is a value judgment on his part and therefore culturally determined in so far as it is determined at all. The same applies to the sufficiency of the inducement offered to whoever extends him credit. Thus the time horizon or the depth of capital in any system of exchanges is culturally determined in this same way and involves a value component. In fact the initiative, ruthlessness, and rationality exercised by the entrepreneur in seeking out and creating opportunities for profit will involve a similar cultural component. The determinants of the bias of culture, however, were not explicitly explored by Innis until after 1940 and may be omitted from the present discussion, though it is well to note where the opening for that discussion was left. To continue, if the entrepreneur is engaged in a purely commercial deal it will involve simply buying cheap and selling dear. If the exchange involves technical transformation of the goods purchased then the deal may be referred to as *industrial*. Now, although this distinction is technical rather than economic, Innis assumed that, in the main, an increase in the proportion of industrial activities would have the economic effect of capital deepening. It is at this point, therefore, in his treatment of growth that he relates technical change to economic change, that is to say development to growth theory. The relation, based on the assumption that technological advance is embodied, was made in the following way. In an industrial deal the profit rate is a function of the cost of inputs, given the operative technique of production, and the selling price of the product. The transformation process in an industrial deal will generally take longer than in a commercial deal and the more sophisticated the technique of transformation the longer it will take again and, therefore, the greater the proportion of industrial deals and the more advanced the technique the more distant the time horizon and the larger the implied surplus must be.

If we accept Innis' distinction between commercial and industrial pursuits as hanging precisely on the degree of technical sophistication in the process of transformation, then in an industrial deal the structure of costs will be characterized more by fixed than by variable elements. That is to say, a larger proportion of total cost will fall under the category of overhead to be paid off over an extended period of primary transactions. The increase in overhead is concomitant with a lengthening of time horizons, both being associated with rigidities in the structure of prices and uncertainties as to profit. In cases involving untried equipment, resources, or markets the uncertainties of taste as expressed in the consensus of values are joined by further uncertainties, making possible changes in the structure of prices even more vexatious to the entrepreneur. But even beyond this more problems arise from the credit-money element in the system. Extension of credit is an activation or creation of surpluses existing in the community. Perhaps one should say that the availability of liquidity is the institutional expression of one limit to capital accumulation. In the normal or usual course of events, depending on the system's degree of inertia in the face of opportunities for profits and inducements to lend, an increase in transactions concomitant with the activation of surpluses will tend to raise the general level of prices. That is to say, a general increase in liquidity tends, in the usual case, to raise prices. Conversely a decrease in liquidity through a withdrawal of credit tends to lower prices. Thus, with uneven stimulation to economic activity and an uneven response, fluctuations in the general level of prices add to the uncertainties already mentioned.

In any case, putting aside the problem of uncertainties for the moment, it is evident that, on Innis' presumptions, the spatial and temporal dimensions of a price system are inter-related. Clearly the spatial extent of the market depends on the efficiency of transportation. Transportation, as one element in the general transformation of goods, will be related from a technical point of view to the general level of sophistication of the industrial arts throughout the system. If, therefore, advance in the industrial arts involves a lengthening of time horizons, a spatial extension of the market following improvements in the technique of transportation will involve a lengthening of the temporal dimension of the price system.

Now, the general state of the industrial arts is related directly to the phenomenon described by Adam Smith as the division of labour. The advantage to an entrepreneur of further division of labour is, usually, a reduction in per unit cost of production and a consequent increase in profits. It is not, of course a division of labour in the sense that one labourer works separated from another, as one farmer works separated or divided from another. Rather it is a concentration of labour in that sense and a division of employments or tasks. Commonly the concentration of labour is occasioned by the introduction of machinery about which the workers are employed so that the advance of technology and the division of labour in the usual case move together. According to Smith, however, the division of labour is limited by the extent of the market. Here the implication is that if the market is not sufficiently large increased overhead cost will not be offset by an increased sales volume even with the possible reduction in price per unit. In the extreme, Smith's argument assumes the pre-existence of a market and a continuous improvement of technique on the part of individual entrepreneurs who have an eye to exploiting its size. If, however, the extent of the market is determined by the efficiency of the technique of communication, as he implies in most of the argument of book I, chapter 3, and this is intimately related to the general state of technique, then it would seem that the advance of technique with its concomitant division of labour would precede and be the occasion of the extension of the market. When fully elaborated this inconsistency leads to two basic questions in development theory. First, does the emergence of a surplus precede or follow technological advance? Second, does the advance of agriculture precede or succeed the advance of industry? Does the improvement of the country precede the improvement of the town? Smith answered these questions one way and Innis answered them the other.

For Smith the 'natural' sequence was prior development of the country. This he considered to be the actual sequence of events in the American colonies, accounting for their rapid advance over the relative stagnation of Europe where the sequence was reversed. Innis, with his eye mainly on the peripheral Canadian economy, disagreed and made use of the confusions of the argument of book I, chapter 3 to refute Smith.

Expansion in the North American colonies as in Europe was the 'cause and occasion of the improvement and cultivation of the country.' Adam Smith in his division of labour based on the extent of the market as determined by transportation can be quoted in support of this suggestion ... The improvement of transportation facilitated expansion of internal and external trade.[2]

2 Innis, 'Significant Factors in Canadian Economic Development,' *Essays in Canadian Economic History* (1956), 201–202.

For Innis space and time (the spatial and temporal dimensions) in a price system were most fruitfully considered as derivatives of the technique of communication.

With the advance of technique thus established as the engine of growth Innis proceeded to explore the accommodating adjustments of the price system. Economic improvement through technical change means lowered costs, an extended market and changed time horizons. It comes about through a general increase in liquidity as entrepreneurs mobilize resources to capitalize on the concomitant increase in opportunities for profit. Areas of high profits become low pressure areas in the economic system into which, born on the winds of liquidity, resources sweep with cyclonic force. For example, in regard to the north west Atlantic, 'New England was a low pressure economic area to which labour and capital were drawn, leaving high pressure areas such as Newfoundland to draw on grades of labour that were poorer and accustomed to lower standards of living.'[3]

In this cyclonic equilibration process the essential elements are technical mobility and financial liquidity. Without freedom to move from high to low pressure areas no adjustment to technical advance is possible. Still, as the advance of technique causes an ever increasing rate of growth, particularly in frontier areas, the proportion of costs falling in the category of fixed overhead also builds up at an ever increasing rate. More specifically, increasing rigidities follow upon the lengthening of time horizons as capital is committed in the form of more sophisticated technique, and thus the continued advance of industrialization means an ever more rapid advance into increasingly irreversible positions. Reverse is economically impossible until the termination of the deals and the realization of expected returns. When such reverses and the implied economic losses are threatened by new advances in technique the entrepreneurial response is to take political action to maintain position and even continue the advance along the obsolescent lines in which there is a vested interest. Depending on the existing technical and economic constraints, on the one hand, and the efficiency of political and military action on the other, a degree of success may be attained in

3 Innis, *The Cod Fisheries* (1940), 152.

reversing the economic adjustment. But improved technique increases political and military efficiency as it creates a situation in which impending losses can only be prevented by military or political action. The prospects for a purely economic equilibrium grow increasingly dim.

Political action divides mainly into two alternative strategies; direct controls to prevent a shift of resources into new low pressure areas, and the creation of an offsetting low pressure area. The creation of offsetting low pressure along established lines implies an entrepreneurial act of breaking through the existing technical and institutional framework of the system and it means planned growth in the now orthodox sense of that term. In an international price system, what emerges is a series of strategic disequilibrating acts on the part of different groups intending to offset or even reverse what may be described as the attempt of opposing groups to do the same thing in their own favour. As these actions and counter actions reveal themselves in the conflict of groups struggling to prevent economic equilibrium through political control of mobility and liquidity, the simple metaphor of cyclonic equilibration becomes inadequate.

We seem destined in economics to follow the meteorologist in modifying equilibrium analysis and turning to what has been called the polar front theory in which the meeting of economic masses becomes important rather than trade between nations. There are serious weaknesses in the analogy of flowing from high pressure to low pressure areas, and advantages in discussing pressure groups. The economics of losses is not less significant than the economics of profits.[4]

In historical fact, as Innis saw the matter, the growth process had followed upon either technological advance or the discovery of precious metals. Both cases involve an increase in liquidity but in different and possibly compensating ways. In what Innis called the *normal* case growth is a consequence of improvements in industrial technique, particularly as it affects transport and communications

4 Innis, 'The Penetrative Powers of the Price System,' in *Essays in Canadian Economic History* (1956), 272.

in general. Improvements result in the transference of capital to marginal areas for the purpose of applying available technique to newly available resources. Both deepening and widening of capital are involved. Where the technique is advanced and capital deepening is pronounced the pay-off period is relatively long and the advance will be followed by a persistent, long-run tendency for liquidity to be drained back from the marginal area in the form of profits and dividends. During the period of development the frontier becomes an extremely liquid low pressure area. 'The economies of frontier countries are the storm centres of the modern international economy.'[5] Following the initial burst of activity in which the relatively heavy overhead is set up, rigidities become increasingly evident amid depressed conditions. Thus, 'normally' the price system deepens and widens in a boom and collapse sequence following technical advance. But discovery of precious metals on the frontier provides liquidity without technical improvements, reversing the usual sequence of events. Liquidity appears in the marginal area without being transferred from the centre. Profits induce capital widening, and even deepening, as innovation follows an upswing in economic activity.

It [the Klondike gold rush] brought a reversal in the trend of a spread of money from the centre to the circumference in the sudden emergence of money on the fringes. Mercantile systems which favoured devices increasing imports of specie and accentuated the importance of liquidity preference were outstripped by the production of large quantities of gold. ... Distortion by the gold rushes of more normal trends of metropolitan development ... in which improved technique in transport and communication gradually led to changes in types of product from the hinterlands, more easily handled products being replaced by less easily handled products, fur by timber and timber by grain ... by speeding up transportation improvement with construction of transcontinental railways.[6]

5 Innis, 'The Political Implications of Unused Capacity,' in *Political Economy in the Modern State* (1946), 228.
6 Innis, 'Liquidity Preference as a Factor in Industrial Development,' in *Essays in Canadian Economic History* (1956), 357.

In these 'normal trends of metropolitan development,' institutional formation played its role after the innovation of new instruments at the centre and before the granting of credit to new areas on the margin. Technical advance merely makes profit possible and organization is necessary to facilitate exploitation of the possibilities. In other words, the development of new institutions is undertaken with a view to adjusting the price system to the demands of new equipment. An efficient price system is one that rapidly mobilizes resources and Innis concluded from his historical work that 'institutional organization had been designed to enhance mobility.'[7] Specifically, in the normal sequence of growth, institutional adjustment is an essential part of the process of equilibration. With the advance of industrialization, however, the normal sequence of growth is replaced by an abnormal institutional ratchet effect. The writing off of monetary and physical organization becomes extremely costly, often virtually impossible. Under the threat of such adjustments, planned mobilization of resources is extended to offset forces working for equilibrium by ensuring continued advance along existing lines. In short, institutions, once established, tend to direct growth rather than be directed by it. (Innis did not make a note of the parallel between this case and that of the discovery of gold on the frontier.) This in turn demands a degree of economic isolation on the part of organizations seeking to thwart 'normal' growth tendencies. The relatively easy adjustments that had been characteristic of the commercial era in North America were reversed by national policies adopted to meet the demands of industrialism and, in consequence, there was a general 'decline in the efficiency of instruments essential in equilibrium.'[8]

Innis' theory of government enterprise is essentially a theory of disequilibrium growth, of an explosive growth path based on economic isolation – a theory of the decline of the price system as described by Adam Smith. Individualism is replaced by nationalism and decentralized decision-making by central planning. In Innis' view each of the new governments established by the peace treaties

7 Innis, *Settlement and the Mining Frontier* (1936), 268.
8 Innis, 'The Decline in the Efficiency of Instruments Essential in Equilibrium' (1953).

following the first world war was, like the Canadian government of 1867, a credit instrument designed to enhance the efficiency of the price system in the mobilization of capital. With national governments thus being an inherent part of the overhead of economic growth, and in the absence of machinery for international bankruptcy, technological change induced them to reverse their role by adopting policies of economic isolation, forced growth and 'all the complex machinery of economic nationalism.'[9]

The problem, of course, was not new. During the mercantilist era the uncertainties that accompanied the use of slower and less reliable means of transport had called forth political action and organization in the form of tariffs, bounties, state monopolies, and the like. When the institutional structure of those empires was dismantled in the nineteenth century, investments initiated in marginal areas under protection were left in an extremely exposed position. To meet their long term commitments these areas were forced to create a political infrastructure that would perform the protective role that previously was performed by mercantilist empires. 'The success of *laissez-faire* has been paid for by the exploited areas of which we are one. And the necessity of developing nationalization in Canada to support Liberalism in Great Britain and the United States raises some interesting questions.'[10] Partly as a result of the ravages of economic storms and partly in an attempt to harness their cyclonic force, marginal areas of the modern international economy had been forced to undertake the economic burden and the institutional support of general economic progress.

9 Innis, 'Economic Nationalism' (1934), 30.
10 Innis, a comment published in *The State and Economic Life* (1934), 289–90.

5

The problem of values
in the Canadian case

The early sketches of cyclonic theory did not feature the value component in economic growth, but after applying the theory in analysis of contemporary problems it became impossible for Innis to avoid the general debate about proper remedies for the depression. His consequent involvement in the market for political opinions so impressed him with the pervasive character of the value component in the alleged fact and theory of political economy that he was impelled to hammer out a substantially new answer to the questions raised by Veblen and debated by Knight and Tugwell.

According to the cyclonic conception, the Canadian government's involvement in the growth process was the derivative of a number of demands for rapid expansion. The strongest demand grew out of a commitment to canals and railways in the St Lawrence drainage basin where the predominance of fixed costs meant vulnerability to technical advances in the competing New York system. Every improvement made in New York had to be matched, or the whole Canadian investment would be lost. At the same time, however, every improvement increased the proportion of overhead costs and the consequent possibility of losses. In the typical case improvement meant rapid acceleration of business activity as the overhead requirement of new areas was built up. When the initial stage of expansion was completed it was generally found that the market was too small for profitable operation at competitive prices and further expansion was necessary. Bursts of expansion associated with heavy overhead and excess capacity were reinforced by a number of related factors. (1) Settlers accustomed to life in developed areas insisted on the immediate realization of advanced living standards. (2) The importance of the communication system in building up new areas created a last link effect. That is to say, when the last link in a long chain of communication came at an intermediate point the consequences of the entire system became evident at once as gaps in available goods and services were suddenly filled. (3) Apparent success in early stages of the whole process, coming in a general upswing of business activity, created a mood of confidence that led to uninhibited investment. (4) In any scheme of expansion based on the application of advanced technique to virgin resources, facilities are installed with a view to gradually building up markets. For some time after the expansion is undertaken, overhead is by far the most important element in cost structure. In other words, expenses are heavily grouped in initial stages of development. (5) In Canada this last factor was exaggerated by the physical characteristics of the terrain and by the severe climate.

The rapidity and amount of investment necessitated by these demands were more than private enterprise could handle. From one point of view it simply failed to meet demand. From another, it was unable to manage the uncertainties involved. Business interests were forced to adopt governmental forms of enterprise. Putting Innis' position as simply as possible, to protect itself against political and economic incursions from the United States and to mobilize credit for expansion, private enterprise, through the colonial governments, created the federal government of Canada to be a common instrument for mobilizing capital. That is to say, the weaknesses of private enterprise as an institutional support for rapid accumulation under conditions of uncertainty, and the general weakness of the price system in organizing a retreat from positions of long-term capital commitment, were overcome by the instruments of government enterprise.

The consequent disequilibrating ratchet of national expansion was self-accelerating. Credit creation required centralization of

economic life and centralization, in turn, accentuated the rigidity
that had been the source of the initial pressure for national expansion. The costs of nation building – for example the costs of non-
commercial railway lines demanded by areas entering confederation
– added to the proportion of fixed overhead in the economy. In fact
all projects undertaken directly by the government, being backed by
the power to tax, were characterized by a larger than normal proportion of capital costs; and private enterprise, using government
guaranteed credit, indulged in heavy capital outlays. The weaknesses
of a commercial price system were remedied by an industrial price
system in which taxes, in part, replaced profits, but the industrial
price system had weaknesses of its own. During the upswing of
business there was success and prosperity but in the downswing the
pressure of debt became unbearable. There was some scaling down
of debts in Canada but most of the debt was owned outside the
country and secured with government guarantees. In the absence of
international bankruptcy provisions adequate relief through the
writing off of debts was out of the question. The only way out was
further expansion based on a more thorough centralization of economic activity. In the beginning, business had created government,
but in a period of depression rigidities in cost structure necessitated
government ownership of those enterprises which had been supported, or of those which had been disadvantaged because others
had been supported. Nationalization was cumulatively intensified.

In the context of this analysis Innis stated the question facing the
Canadian economist.

What are the results of a situation in which the profit index ceases to
operate or operates too efficiently, and the engineer is allowed to run
loose, so that the swiftness of development and its unpredictable character are beyond the scope of normal economic theory?[1]
It belongs to an essentially dynamic or cyclonic development.[2]
The usual economic practice breaks down ... we become involved in a
study of economic pathology.[3]

1 Innis 'Snarkov Island,' 5. See also p. 148 below.
2 Innis, 'The Economic Destiny of Canada,' 6.
3 'Snarkov Island,' 6. See also p. 148 below.

[A] new country, especially Canada, cannot afford to rely on the theory
borrowed from old industrialized countries but she must attack with all
the skill and industry she can command the task of working out a
theory adapted to the situation in which she is able to defend herself
against exploitation, against the drawing off of her large resources and
against violent fluctuations which are characteristic of exploitation without after thought.[4]

The Canadian problem was the problem of planned growth. Its
roots stretched back to the days of the fur trade, but its contemporary manifestation in the depression could be traced to the inauguration of the National Policy of 1878. That plan involved the mobilization of capital to yield a profit of sufficient size to pay off the debt
incurred and to provide for continued operation and expansion of
the projects undertaken. A sufficiently large profit was ensured by
the ready availability of advanced technique and virgin resources.
The difficulty lay in attracting the necessary capital while at the
same time securing Canadian ownership. More precisely, it was a
question of how to cut out the Canadian share to ensure payment of
the debt and continued expansion. Innis thought of the tariff as the
only feasible means to this end. In the past land sales to settlers and
direct taxation of natural resources had proven inoperable. The
excess profits tax was 'notoriously unsuccessful.'

We are forced to turn to other devices in this pathological study. Our
only alternative is revenue secured from the tariff. How can we adjust
the tariff so that, among other things, the interest rate to be paid on
capital for building railroads will be paid by those industries which have
gained from construction of railroads? This is a question more easily
asked than answered. However we may suggest certain possibilities. We
may confidently leave to the railways the question of ways and means
of exploitation. How can we guarantee that we shall get a reasonable
share of the abnormal profits which accompany the exploitation of
natural resources so that we can at least pay the interest on the capital
we have borrowed to construct the railways and perhaps pay off some

4 *Ibid.*, 9. See also p. 149 below.

of the mortgage? ... The alternative is of course the tariff on machinery and equipment used for exploitation. A carefully adjusted tariff may make it possible to skim off a substantial portion of the cream by taxing equipment, raising costs of production and thereby reducing profits which would otherwise flow off into the hands of foreign investors.[5]

During the period of initial expansion the tariff had been a passable success. In the subsequent contraction it became a hindrance to necessary adjustment. In any period, in fact, it had been at best 'a crude device' from a number of points of view. Here again Innis saw the main problem in terms of the ratchet-like forces working for continued expansion. Government support of industry had been financed by tariff revenues with the initial rates set at reasonable levels for revenue purposes. But they remained at these levels, inflexible downward, both at the peak of expansion and in the following depression. At the peak, surplus revenues became the occasion of over confidence and over expansion. In the subsequent period of depression, the tariff changed in nature, becoming primarily protective and adding to the burden of the debt. To remedy these shortcomings Innis recommended a 'scientific tariff' that would be higher in periods of prosperity, increased revenues being a means of withdrawing capital from new projects for the sake of paying the debt on old projects. It would prevent excessive expansion and reduce foreign debt. In periods of depression the 'scientific tariff' would be lowered to reduce the burden of the debt.

Granting that the tariff was an efficient tax wedge Innis raised the question as to whether its incidence was in fact on the share of the foreign capitalist. 'The ultimate question of borrowing becomes one of determining the incidence of the tariff.'[6] He was aware that much of the incidence had fallen on consumers in outlying areas, particularly in the Maritimes and on the prairie. During prosperous times the workings of the scheme were not apparent. All producers in the West, for instance, were then infra-marginal and capable of carrying the burden on a padding of profit. In depressed times the point of incidence became painfully evident. Other elements in the economy,

5 *Ibid.*, 7–8. See also pp. 148–9 below.
6 'The Economic Destiny of Canada,' 5.

some consumers and some industrial workers, in consequence of an uneven intensity of competition, found themselves in the same exposed position. In short, the tariff scheme for economic growth may have been successful in gaining some growth, but at the price of an unfortunate distribution of the burden. There were, of course, some offsetting compensations. The outlying areas had the benefit of subsidized transportation, the subsidy drawn from the tariff revenues. Moreover, and perhaps primarily, there were the benefits of faster development. On the whole, abstracting from the broad problems of cumulative rigidity and centralization of power, Innis concluded that the scheme had not worked well, but it had worked.

Whatever sort of qualified success the tariff may have been in achieving growth, its existence implied that the presupposed realities of neoclassical value theory either had never existed in Canada or had been removed as a matter of deliberate policy. The values sought in the economy did not reflect market commodity or time preferences in a theoretically orthodox sense. Social value judgments had been made in the achievement of growth in the past and they would have to be made increasingly in the future. For Innis the whole of Canadian history after 1840 was one 'long period of economic planning.'[7] As for the future:

The price level has become a far from delicate indicator in adjusting supply and demand ... We are faced with problems of overhead cost on a vast scale, prices have become less satisfactory as indicators, the solution depends on the introduction of economic intelligence which avoids monopoly and perfect competition ... nationalism with intelligence ... an intelligent dictator (e.g. civil service) preferred.[8]

Despite his belief in the need for social policy and 'the inevitability of planning,' Innis had serious doubts about quick and easy solutions to the problems to be solved. The economy was 'pathological' but 'the state of the social sciences [would] not support the arguments of those who [favoured] the introduction of straight jackets.'[9]

7 Innis, 'Government Ownership and the Canadian Scene,' in *Essays in Canadian Economic History* (1956), 81–2.
8 Innis, *The Canadian Economy and Its Problems* (1934), 24.
9 *Ibid.*, 24.

The concept of planning meant an explicit role for social value judgments, which are arrived at through some political process. Planning for growth, however, could mean either aggressive policies or conservative policies, because a zero growth rate is still a growth rate. Innis' hope was to rectify the errors of the aggressive growth policies of the past. Where previous attempts to increase the growth rate had led to centralization and government enterprise Innis wanted to decentralize planning as much as possible to the provincial level and to construct a strategic balance between government and private enterprise. He wanted to offset the inevitable rigidities of planning by some recourse to older forms of the price system. On the federal level he proposed a three-way division of planning between the Board of Railway Commissioners, the Tariff Board and a central government bank. Within this institutional framework he suggested a programme that would proceed along four main lines.[10]

1 Checks on the growth of the burden of the debt: (a) reduced government spending; (b) rationalized control of government debt; (c) control of corporate securities; (d) restriction of immigration.

2 Extension of powers to adjust the burden of the debt: (a) the Tariff Board and the Board of Railway Commissioners balancing the burden between industrial and agricultural areas; (b) Combines Investigation Act machinery to reduce price spreads; (c) increased income tax; (d) Industrial Disputes Investigation Act extended to protect labour; (e) support for marketing co-operatives; (f) improved machinery for relief of unemployment.

3 Reduction of the burden of the debt: (a) reduction of interest on government debts by tax or conversion; (b) machinery for scaling down debts and reducing interest rates.

4 Strengthening support for the burden of the debt: (a) continued attempts to increase international trade; (b) reduction of costs through research; (c) reduction of political interference with banking; (d) a search for avenues through which to attract foreign capital.

10 The following is condensed from *Problems of Staple Production in Canada* (1933), vii-ix.

The evident peculiarities of this programme are its stress on reduction and adjustment of the debt, and its conservative approach to growth. Its not so evident peculiarity is that it *is* an approach to growth. The programme is drawn up from the point of view of long-run considerations affecting growth and the limits set on growth by the availability of a surplus. Whatever similarities there may have been between the proposals of J.M. Keynes and Innis, this difference stands out. Keynes' proposals were drawn up from the point of view of short-run phenomena consequent on growth and the limits set on employment by an unfortunate use of available surpluses. Both men had conservative policies in regard to growth but in the short run, Keynesian conceptualization it was not as evident. Keynesian expansion would have been largely an increased production of consumer's goods with a view to achieving full employment. It was time to cut the cake, not to make it bigger. This, of course, is not at all the sort of expansion that Innis had in mind and wanted to control, but he failed to see the difference. He had a great fear that would-be theorists, supported by the uninformed enthusiasm of the electorate, would direct the economy back into perverse policies of forced growth. In the context of this fear, which may have been justified by what was happening in Canada, he judged the journalist-politician, Keynes, to be just another promoter of short-run solutions that would only aggravate the long-run problems they were supposed to solve. He put it this way, 'Monetary nationalism is a reflection of the role of the state in the expansion of industrialism and the means by which the state is compelled to rely increasingly on expanded public debt to avoid increasingly its effects.'[11]

The problem seemed to be that, while social value judgments were necessary, there were almost irresistible pressures preventing the greatest possible degree of objectivity in the preparation of such judgments. Here again Innis noted a failure of equilibrating mechanisms with a consequent, cumulative, one-sided development. Economic theories tended to be mere epiphenomena of economic problems, rationalizations of the prejudiced assertions of involved partisans. Granted, 'the welfare of the nation for the future [would]

11 H.A. Innis, 'The Penetrative Powers of the Price System,' in *Essays in Canadian Economic History* (1956), 271.

depend to an increasing extent on the economist,' but contemporary economics was little more than the intellectual dimension of the problems to be solved. The complexity of the problems and the slow growth of economic work have tended to make his [the economist's] contributions of relatively little value. Distribution of the weight of the burden of the debt must still be made by the rough and effective method of political pressure. The political scientist is perhaps more urgently demanded than the economist.'[12]

In Canada the situation seemed to be particularly bad. On top of all the problems of vested interests and rationalization, and the problems inherent in the very idea of objectively scientific economics, there were the additional difficulties arising from the fact that Canada was a new country and had not yet developed an economics of its own. Enormous advantages had been gained from the importation of foreign scholars, but they had been offset by enormous losses. Economists born or trained in developed areas were unaware of the peculiarities of the political economy of the frontier, and their presence in Canada inhibited the emergence of scholars with a more relevant orientation. The general effect was an undue emphasis on the short-run, static, analysis as developed in older countries.

... the whole field of long term credit has been neglected.

... the character of the geographic background, of the industries which emerge from that background, of the cultural characteristics in the social and political institutions of these industries, and of the changes which accompany technological advance and more rapid utilization and exhaustion of natural resources, tends to be neglected in the emphasis on price statistics ... This is not to neglect the significance of the equilibrium approach, the importance of the quantification in economics, but rather to attempt to give them meaning and content.[13]

Granted the classical analysis [was] of fundamental importance, but it [carried] the economist far short of his goal of scientific explanation.[14]

In the midst of all this there was the practical necessity of immediate action.

12 Innis, 'Notes and Comments' (1932), 5.
13 Innis, 'Approaches to Canadian Economic History' (1936), 26.
14 Innis, review of *Wheat* by W.W. Swanson and P.C. Armstrong, and of
    The Canadian Grain Trade by D.A. MacGibbon (1932), 344.

For economists the task is most depressing. The untold misery of the slump has made sustained objective study extremely difficult and has led economists on all sides to desert the subject and flee to politics. The results are disastrous. The modern development of talk has brought the subject to a level at which it is safe to say that any economist with a large political following has almost certainly lowered his colours from the standpoint of a scientific investigation. And yet to say this is to expose oneself to the most bitter attacks on grounds of lacking sympathy with human misery. These are bad days for the economists.[15]

Innis thought that economics should have been as much as possible 'like Caesar's wife, beyond reproach,' but his colleagues had taken to partisan activity, adding to the unrest and becoming themselves part of the problem. They were 'trying to measure the burden [of the debt] by adding their own weight to the scales.' The result, in Innis' reckoning, was the economist's proposal to do again what the politicians had done in the past, to embark on perverse expansionary schemes based on governmental manipulation of credit. Innis could justify such schemes for the early stage of growth but he thought that that stage had passed and that corrective, balancing policies were required. The success of previous schemes had depended on autonomous factors, particularly the possibility of profits resulting from the application of advanced technique to virgin resources. He was certain that similar factors would be important in any return to rapid growth, and that without them monetary and fiscal manipulation by the government was, at best, useless. In the meantime economics seemed to be degenerating into the 'incantation of irrelevancies' as economists rode out the storm in the role of 'travelling comedians appearing at political rallies.'

Our fellow citizen the Eskimo, it is said, often succeeds in bringing back the caribou after a long period of starvation through the efforts of medicine men, and the pronouncements of their more 'educated' brethren are entitled to the same regard in curing the depression ... In the past a medicine man from abroad has been worth about six of the local product ... medicine men from Great Britain tend to be regarded as most potent

15 Innis, review of *The Philosophy of Henry George* by G.R. Geiger (1933), 7.

... [But] evil spirits are not exorcized by an appeal to other evil spirits. They die only with the skepticism which follows a persistent attempt to understand the problems of modern society.[16]

Innis was face to face with the problem of the role of values in economics and he was caught in a dilemma over the matter. In the face of the claims of liberals, his teacher, Frank Knight, had denied the possibility of scientific economics. The head of his department, E.J. Urwick, took the same position as Knight in regard to the possibility of scientific economics, but then chose to support the involvement of academics in liberal movements. Neither was illogical, for the difference between these two, who believed ethics to be the basis of economics, was simply a difference of values. The difference was one of faith, not of reason. Innis accepted this whole situation and then argued that some degree of scientific objectivity was possible in so far as bias or value judgment itself is observable. 'The habits or biases of individuals which permit prediction are re-enforced in the cumulative bias of institutions and constitute the chief interest of the social scientist.'[17] On this showing, persistence or change in economic doctrine implies something about the values organized into society, and the way is open to an economic interpretation of economics. At no point did Innis ever admit to the philosophic principle of determinism, but after 1935 he did attempt to discover the technical and institutional factors in the bias of economics and of economic systems. What has been called 'the later Innis' was the result of this attempt to discover the determinants of the value component of economic systems and it was, therefore, a direct approach to the problematic value component in economic growth. He was exploring what Joan Robinson has called the 'animal spirits' of the capitalists.

16 'Approaches to Canadian Economic History' (1936), 29–30.
17 'The Role of Intelligence' (1935), 283.

6

The role of values
in economic growth

As clearly as Innis had again raised the problem of values, he still did not explicitly organize his research about it. The last years of the depression were a time of gestation. He was convinced that the main lines of Canadian economic history[1] to 1914 had been drawn, though there was still much work to do. For the period after 1914 there were too many unanswered questions to permit definitive generalizations. In research he gave priority to monographs on special topics. He encouraged his students in such work and participated in it himself, though his own interest tended to broaden into politics. Nonetheless, and this is the point, the question of values continued to intrude itself into his thinking until, by 1940, he had explicitly adopted a philosophical position that resolved the dilemma issuing from Veblen's critique of neoclassical value theory.

The persistence with which the question plagued Innis is evident in his treatment of conservation. Prior to 1935 he had consistently pleaded for the conservation of Canadian resources against rapid exploitation to meet the demands of developed areas. When the depression produced 'a spate of literature' on the subject he began to see it in a different light. Perhaps he began to see his own position as a product of the bias of Canadian growth. By 1938 he was treat-

1 The period was marked by the publication of Mrs Innis' *An Economic History of Canada* (Toronto, 1935).

ing conservation propaganda as merely another facet of the institutional ratchet of government planning, as part of the general movement towards nationalism and isolation in economic affairs. There was a value judgment involved in the plea for 'wise use of our resources.'

Efficient conservation, the opposite of 'exploitation without after thought,' was simply a controlled rate of exploitation or planned growth. The plan, or rather the values implied by the plan, received expression in the institutional framework involved, and the institutional framework was in some manner controlled by technological factors. In a revision of *The Fur Trade*[2] Innis carefully documented this process by making the whole story turn on the idea of conservation. When the trade had been organized competitively there had been rapid exploitation, but the limitations of the market for a luxury item and the demands of geography and technology in communication lines forced amalgamation and this facilitated a more rational approach. In other words the consequences of growth and the development of institutions controlling the rate of growth interacted with one another until some equilibrium rate of exploitation emerged. What had been true of the fur trade Innis thought to be true of the general advance of modern industrialism. Putting it directly, the increasing importance of overhead costs consequent upon the technical characteristics of modern industry had led to a greater degree of monopoly or, at least, had suggested the possibilities of centralization for controlling the rate of growth and its consequences. Thus technical constraints, through their effect on institutions, were one factor in the value judgment embodied in the phrase 'The wise use of our resources.' Under the heading of conservation Innis began to cope with the determinants of the value component in growth.

Innis was coming to the assertion that, from one point of view, the rate of growth is controlled by value judgments receiving expression in institutions. That is to say, growth is a cultural phenomenon. From this it followed that any change in the organization of an economy would change its cultural form and the conditions of its

2 Innis, 'Introduction,' in R.H. Fleming (ed.), *Minutes of Council, Northern Department of Rupert Land, 1812–31* (1941).

growth. Having brought his thinking so far during the depression and the war, Innis passed an adverse judgment on the kinds of institutional change that were being made in his own time. He thought always in terms of the self-accelerating bias of centralization that increasingly used growth to overcome its own problems. He became alarmed over losses from the traditions of western civilization, and feared that if they continued western civilization would destroy itself. Just as government support (conservation) in one sector of an economy put other sectors at a disadvantage, so general planning put individual initiative at a disadvantage and implied a failure to conserve the cultural heritage of the West. The important changes bearing on the rate of exploitation were institutional and ultimately a matter of values.

North American exploitation of natural resources has reached the stage in which exhaustion through competition between Canada and the United States has necessitated concentration on conservation and, in turn, co-operation. The increased strength of the executive in the United States ... and of a small group in the Cabinet ... in Canada has facilitated the establishment of joint committees. These developments become tolerable only with concentration on political organization. The task of conservation is not one of technology but of culture.[3]

This same theme ran through Innis' edition of *The Diary of Alexander James McPhail* (Toronto, 1940). Whatever the Wheat Pool had wanted when they commissioned him, Innis turned the diary into a case study in institutional formation. The purpose of the Pool, as it appeared in the account, was to achieve stability in the marketing of grain. That is to say, to eliminate the cycle of alternate rapid exploitation and collapse. The aim was conservation. Innis' selection of texts showed that in the formation of the Pool disagreements had centred on whether or not the organization would be democratic or bureaucratic. That is, the problem of controlled growth expressed itself in conflict over organizational form. Democracy accentuated the importance of flexibility to meet new opportunities whereas bureaucracy accentuated the importance of

3 Innis, 'The Economic Aspect' (1942), 15.

controls to prevent flooding the market. That Innis should select as McPhail's contribution his ability to contain both factions in one institution and make it work was an indication of the direction of Innis' thinking in regard to the character of the value component in growth.

Towards the end of the nineteen-thirties a Royal Commission on Dominion-Provincial Relations (the Rowell-Sirois Commission) examined the economic basis of confederation in order to assess the division of powers between the central and the provincial governments. Innis thought the situation called for a balance of forces, as in the case of the Wheat Pool, but the Commission did not. For Innis the *Report* was the ominous beginning of a new era in Canada.[4] When the problems that the Wheat Pool was supposed to have solved showed up in conflict over the sort of organization the Pool would be, McPhail was there to hold things in balance and make it work. When the same thing happened in connection with the inability of the provinces to co-operate in producing the *Report*, there was no-one like McPhail to remedy the situation. The drafting of the *Report* fell into the hands of academics, particularly economists, who gave it a specious unity that was unrelated to the conflicting value judgments involved. Innis identified the Commission's policy proposals as a type of Keynesian manipulation of national income that could not be carried out without prejudice to democracy in Canada. The basic problem of the tariff, and, in view of regional differences, the relative efficiency of the provinces in social services, were ignored. In place of these considerations there was constructed an artificial division of functions at the national level on the basis of types of needs, while the real need for equilibrium adjustments was ignored in favour of grants to depressed areas. Again it was a case of institutionalizing disequilibrium through a process of centralization and increasing rigidity.

While the logic of Innis' position was relentlessly driving him on to a more explicit treatment of the question of values, some exogenous factors impelled him even more rapidly in that direction. One of the most important of these was the development of instruction in marketing in the School of Commerce at Toronto.

4 Innis, 'The Rowell-Sirois Report' (1940).

Another was a running debate in his own department over the nature of sociology as a social science. There were others too, but for the moment these best illuminate the direction in which Innis was moving.

The course on marketing drew his attention to the importance of advertising in the formation of commodity preferences. He understood its importance both in its direct and indirect effects throughout the broad value infrastructure of economic activity.

Why do business men criticize advertising agencies for their general optimism and lack of constructive criticism? Why do they complain that they sell advertising more effectively than they sell goods? What are the implications of the development of advertising for the growth of art in Canada? What has been the significance to literature? How far does literature in Canada depend on the support of advertising and what are the advantages and disadvantages of this dependence? How far does advertising influence editorial policies and how far does it affect politics directly or indirectly?[5]

He explored the field using the idea of a gap between what he called producer's and consumer's marketing[6] – i.e., marketing from the point of view of the conditions of production and consumption. The idea was not unlike Veblen's theory of the dichotomy between the engineer and the price system, between the instinct of workmanship in production and the predatory instinct in business enterprise. Its main proposition was that technical improvements in transportation and communication had progressively widened the gap between producer's and consumer's marketing until, with the advent of radio and aircraft, the forces involved in consumer's marketing had been given extremely independent play. In Canada a centralized and monopolistic though not vertically integrated marketing structure was evidence of the extremely wide gap characteristic of modern industrialism. In general he was saying that the character and effectiveness of advertising relates the means of communication

5 Innis, 'The Necessity of Research in Marketing' (1940), 13.
6 Innis, 'Foreword,' in Jane McKee (ed.), *Marketing Organization and Techniques* (1940).

to a certain bias in the price system. From this proposition it is no distance at all to the conclusion that the state of the communication arts is an important factor in determining the values that direct distribution and growth. Innis called for 'an aggressive attack on a subject which [had] enormous significance to modern civilization and especially for Canada ...'[7]

The debate over sociology raised again the question of the scientific character of the social sciences. In this case Innis chose to emphasize the value component of the social sciences rather than the possibilities for a scientific approach based on the persistence of bias (values) in individuals and institutions. He could see the place for sociology among the social sciences but he despaired of it ever fitting in. Each of the social sciences, in his view, was biased in favour of the value presuppositions of the institutions that encouraged its growth. The advantage of a new social science, therefore, was its tendency to offset the biases of older social sciences. In Innis' experience, however, establishing a new science in the university involved it in a debasing competition with cognate subjects that rendered it incapable of fulfilling its promise. Added to this, the professors of the new science, coming from different disciplines, would not agree among themselves as to what the new science was all about. Innis himself could see no advantage deriving from clear definitions of each branch of social science and he deplored the propensity of some sociologists to pretend to be the dividers and co-ordinators of all other branches. In this regard he believed the real problem to be that that discipline which should have been the co-ordinator of the social sciences had failed in the task. Philosophy was dead, 'killed, stuffed and properly labeled,' and no social science could substitute for it. Unmistakably Innis was identifying himself with the position taken by Urwick in the debate of 1935. 'Exponents of the individual disciplines of social science, including philosophy, one by one, wash their hands of the problems of philosophy or offer spurious remedies and alternatives. It is a pleasure to refer to the

7 Innis, review of *The Story of Marketing: a Chronicle of Fifty Years* by H.E. Stephenson and C. McNaught, and *The History of an Advertising Agency* by R.M. Hower (1941), 111–12.

work of Professor MacIver, Professor Urwick and others to maintain an interest in the fundamental problems of civilization.'[8]

Innis' praise of Urwick and MacIver is indicative of the effect on him of the controversy about sociology. Further indication may be found in his correspondence. In January, 1942, he exchanged notes with A.G. Huntsman of the department of biology at Toronto concerning C.W.M. Hart's contention that sociology should use an absolutely scientific method, that is that it should start with the methodological presumption that 'the free, rational individual is a myth.'[9] Hart had compared MacIver, a 'liberal sociologist,' to Durkheim, stating that the former presumed personal freedom and the latter did not. *A propos* of this Innis asked Huntsman about the possibility of using the methods of studying animal populations to study sociological phenomena. Huntsman thought they could not be used in the latter case. In July, 1940, Innis overcame the legacy of an old quarrel to begin a lively, if sporadic, correspondence with Urwick. Urwick's replies pertained to Innis' troubles with sociology and to Urwick's new book on values[10] which he thought would have the sympathy of Innis and F.H. Knight.

Perhaps one has to accept the proposition that there is no complete explanation of Innis' decision to make values the prime concern of his research. At some point, no doubt prodded by circumstances and led by logic, he simply chose to take the direction in which he went. By the same token it is difficult to explain completely his interest in classics. It may have been logic, for his interest in the rise and fall of civilizations would lead him to study classical culture. It may have been circumstance, for in 1940 the University of Toronto was certainly the centre of classical studies in North America. Perhaps it was choice. Whatever it was, once Innis began reading C.N. Cochrane's *Christianity and Classical Culture*[11] his interest in values and the determinants of values was confirmed.

8 Innis, *Empire and Communications* (1950), 11.
9 C.W.M. Hart, 'Some Obstacles to a Scientific Sociology,' in C.W.M. Hart (ed.), *Essays in Sociology* (Toronto, 1940), 36–52.
10 E.J. Urwick, *The Values of Life*, ed. A. Irving (Toronto, 1948).
11 For Innis' own review of Cochrane's work see 'Charles Norris Cochrane' (1946).

Cochrane's analysis of Graeco-Roman culture led to the conclusion that that civilization had disintegrated as a result of its inability to resolve a conflict of values, the tragic conflict between virtue and fate. Christianity, however, transcended the problem by insisting, in the Nicene Creed, that being and becoming are one. (Thus Cochrane interpreted the concept of the trinity in which the three persons are asserted to be one god.) For Christian civilization, the values and the institutions, there was no fundamental dichotomy between order and change (form and process) (virtue and fate), or between the so-called Apollonian and Dionysian elements in life. Granted there was a logical contradiction between them but, as in the case of the one-in-three doctrine, Christianity transcended the problems of mathematical logic, the conflict being resolved, according to Cochrane, in the creative response of individuals who somehow rise above both formal logic and the social forms of human behaviour. The doctrine pointed to a 'philosophy of dynamic personality' in which the creativity of the individual rather than formalistic science or irrational democracy was the key to civilization's survival and advance. Applying this to his own day Cochrane rejected both socialism and fascism, which he related respectively to emotion and science (Dionysian and Apollonian elements), and made a plea for a creative individualism that would transcend the problems inherent in the other two.

The importance of this highly speculative thesis for Innis' work cannot be doubted. Certainly it is as important as the 1940 lecture of R.E. Park, to which Marshall McLuhan has pointed.[12] Park took a position that left room for both a scientific approach to the study of values and for putting limits on the usefulness of that approach. He reasserted the old Veblenian doctrine of the role of communications in directing social activity, but he also insisted on the importance of the individual in bringing about advance by breaking through the limitations of social action as dictated by custom and technical constraints. In the process of the advance of civilization Park relegated science to a 'merely secondary and instrumental' role and he put emphasis on the importance of what

12 H.M. McLuhan, 'Introduction,' in Innis, *The Bias of Communication* (Toronto, 1965).

he called philosophy and religious faith. In effect he was restating Innis' own position but making it more explicit by including the indeterminate moral assertiveness of the human subject. In short, there was here a suggestion that the Veblenian analysis be retained except for the instinct hypothesis, for which there should be substituted the hypothesis of indeterminate creative individualism.

Where then did this leave the original problem of the causes of economic progress? Veblen had overcome the weaknesses of preceding theories of growth by explaining the emergence of a surplus in terms of costless technological advance. (We may add to this an Innisian factor, costless institutional advance.) But the Veblenian doctrine, running entirely in terms of efficient causality, had been unable to cope with the remaining problem, that is, how new techniques and institutions emerged from the constraints of the old. By 1940 Innis had decided that that problem could not be solved except in terms of some idea of creative individualism. Ultimately the explanation of growth reduced to a matter of indeterminate moral assertion and, therefore, was by nature pre-scientific. What was left for scientific explanation was the extent to which the constraints of environment allowed creativity room for play in one direction or another. The history of the advance of civilization did not ultimately explain the advance but recounted the interaction of constraints with the exploration of values. The problem of growth reduced itself to the problem of values for which, in the Innisian scheme of things there is no resolution.

7

The role of values in
the nature and history
of social science

The assertion that economic progress has a pre-scientific and a pre-logical aspect created a place for politics in Innis' theory of growth and gave him a vantage point from which he was able to see all the elements of social science in inter-relation. It put him in an intellectual position to write his 'economic history of economics.' While he was doing this he began to explore the effects of communication media as the technological determinants of the values relevant to the growth process. Either of these undertakings would have been enough to fill a lifetime but he attempted both of them with less than half of his life to run. The sort of conclusions to which he came in the communications studies are the subject of the next chapter. His analysis of the development of social science is the subject of the present one.

As Innis understood it each branch of social science had developed under the protection of some institution whose existence it rationalized. Hence the specialization, bias and disequilibrium of the institutions of modern civilization were reflected in the appearance of these characteristics in modern social science. The division of labour in society had resulted in an unfortunate division of labour in the social sciences, with each division ignoring the existence and importance of the others. Contrary to this development, Innis insisted on the existential unity and interaction of every element in human behaviour. At every stage of analysis there had to be explicit recognition of the validity of all points of view. Perhaps some sort of competition between the different divisions would ensure a well-rounded view, but the sort of competition that did exist led every branch to claim for itself the irrefutable truth of a natural science, and thus all were led to deny any place for values and to deny the radically indeterminate and pre-scientific character of social science itself.

The clearest statement of Innis' position in regard to the nature of social science is his presidential address to the Economic History Association,[1] but even there he did not set it out with complete logical rigour. Gaps were left in the framework of the presentation and repeated applications to the history of economic thought make it necessary for the reader to extract an already difficult notion from the complexity of particular examples. To reconstruct the doctrine it is necessary to reduce the richness of Innis' style and to supplement the presidential address with references to other statements that he made on the subject.[2]

According to the statement in the address social science has four focal points of interest, each relating to a particular insight and mode of procedure. At one extreme geography, demography and the history of technology deal with the physical limitations within which human behaviour takes place. Geography is the purest type at this extreme, since it is concerned almost exclusively with physical quantities and is largely descriptive in its mode of procedure. It comes closest to being a natural rather than a social science.[3] At the other extreme, philosophy and cultural history deal with human activity from the point of view of values. Philosophy, the purest type in this case, proceeds by insight and deduction.[4] Between the extremes of geography and philosophy, social science has two

1 Innis, 'On the Economic Significance of Cultural Factors,' in *Political Economy in the Modern State* (1946).
2 A second fairly complete statement may be found in his 'In the Tradition of Dissent' (1943).
3 See also Innis, 'Geography and Nationalism' (1945), 304.
4 See also Innis, review of *A Study of War* by Quincy Wright (1943), 597. The phrase 'proceeds by insight and deduction' has been added here for the sake of logical completion. The most Innis said on this point was that values are indeterminate.

other focal points of interest, each being an extreme in another logical dimension. These are two principles of social organization: coercion, which is the principle of politics; and exchange, which is the principle of economics. Politics, dealing with institutions, proceeds largely by the historical method.[5] Economics, dealing with society from the point of view of price, proceeds largely by way of logical elaboration or mathematics.

The whole thing can be put differently and more completely by stating that Innis postulated a six-dimensional concept of social action and then dealt with the interaction of social phenomena as seen from the point of view of each dimension. By clear implication this interaction involved two independent factors, physical constraints and values. The former was considered determinate in itself but significant only when it entered into relation with phenomena having an element of indeterminateness.[6] The latter was in some sense radically indeterminate, and significant because it was indeterminate, though at any point of time operating within some physical limits. In the context of these two principles (determinateness and indeterminateness, i.e. physical constraints and aspirations) social action took place in terms of two more principles, calculated exchange and coercive power, i.e. co-operation and force. Cutting across the interaction of these four principles were two more principles or dimensions, space and time. The time dimension was dealt with in terms of 'long run' and 'short run' considerations, and the space dimension in terms of centralization and decentralization. Thus there were two polar tendencies in each of the space and time dimensions, and in each of the other four dimensions or principles there was a particular set of concepts to represent one or both of the two antithetical or polar tendencies: in politics, power and freedom; in economics, monopoly and competition; in philosophy, reason and emotion; in religion, dogma and dissent; and technology and geography had their peculiar biases in both space and time.

Innis' use of these concepts was by no means consistent. Indeed, some of his literary effects were derived from mixing and correlating

5 Innis was aware of a new kind of behavioural political science.
  See *ibid.*, 598.
6 See also Innis, 'Social Sciences, Brief Survey of Recent Literature'
  (1942), xi.

concepts: for example, 'monopoly of knowledge' as applied to religious organization, or 'Cartels and formalism in commerce parallelled ecclesiasticism in religion and in both cases initiative in thought was weakened. Volumes of economic history were written about business, epitaphs in two volumes [George Moore], as part of the literature of the new scriptures.'[7] Followed by the intriguing sentence, 'Ecclesiasticism and the devastating effects of the depression brought on acute paralysis of thought and then the rush to such illusions and catchwords as security and full employment.' The style packed his words with meaning for anyone who understood, and made them a source of baffling intrigue and startling discovery for the uninitiated. C.R. Fay once sent a card to Innis on which was written, 'History a la Innis, Cod Fisheries, p. 212. Top. "The influence of the imperialism of Rome and the Mediteranean made itself felt in the destruction of Republican institutions and the birth of Christ, A.D. 1." '[8]

In this frame of reference, and in this style, Innis wrote his brief history of the social sciences.[9] It was in effect a history of every element of social science told in terms of anecdotes and citations that changed his point of view almost at random, sometimes within the span of a single sentence. Any unity in presentation lay in the total picture composed of the inter-related elements and insights. The following précis, hopefully, will be faithful to his meaning though it will lack the excitement of his style.

Political economy came into definitive existence at the time of Adam Smith when there was a balance of power between church, state, and popular opinion. The balance began to emerge when Luther asserted the right to dissent from church dogma. Following the Reformation there was a nationalist alliance of church and state that placed both the principle of value and the principle of coercion under unified control. Calvin's contribution was to give these two principles independent play by insisting on separation of church

7 Innis, 'On the Economic Significance of Cultural Factors' (1946), 97.
8 C.R. Fay to Innis (Feb. 7, 1940).
9 Most of the material constituting this phase of Innis' work was published in the volume of essays, *Political Economy in the Modern State* (Toronto, 1946). Some good additional material may be found in 'The Passing of Political Economy' (1938).

and state. With the state thus losing one of the supports of nationalism, the nationalistic policies of mercantilism began to crumble before the free-trade predilections of commercial interests, and parliament, the voice of the latter, began to encroach on the crown. From the point of view of values, the puritanism of parliament began to encroach on the doctrines of the established church. Then, with the effects of the age of enlightenment, more emotional attitudes began to lose ground to reason and a balanced approach became possible. About this same time the union of England and Scotland was achieved and circumstances were ripe for the emergence of Adam Smith and a well-rounded political economy. *'The Wealth of Nations* was an enquiry into the nature and causes of a broad cultural character.'[10]

Almost immediately after Adam Smith the balance of forces was lost and political economy began a progressive decline into bias and disunity. The universities, the purveyors of newer streams of thought and progressive points of view, continued to gain ground against the restrictions of both church and state. As a result, the sort of political economy that became fashionable was one which replaced rather than incorporated theology; and theology, left on its own, became the conservative support of vested interests in church and state organizations. All the while commercial interests continued to press mercantilist interests in the economic sphere with a consequent demand for new forms of governmental organization and for the intellectual means to justify them. The latter was accomplished by abandoning the older philosophical point of view in favour of the demographic and biological point of view as the hedonistic ethic, social Darwinism, and similar doctrines became the implicit or explicit preconceptions of political economy.

Towards the end of the nineteenth century socialist forces made serious encroachments on the place of commercial interests. The socialists, in their turn, exploited those aspects of social science that tended to favour their position, particularly theories built up from the technological point of view and from the point of view of coercion. As the socialists stressed change, growth, institutional adjustment and the onward march of history; commercial interests were

10 Innis, 'The Passing of Political Economy' (1938), 4.

forced to rely solely on the hedonistic calculus and modern 'value theory' was elaborated on the basis of this abstraction. Unfortunately the hedonistic calculus or utilitarian ethic was, in fact, no ethic at all, but a device that substituted the logic of rationalist calculation for value judgment. Thus, when economics separated itself from the other social sciences at the end of the nineteenth century it was a mere discipline of timeless and morally vacuous mathematical calculation. In fact, all the social sciences – economic history, institutional economics, sociology, constitutional history, and behaviouralist political science – developed into mere specialties in such a way that the insight of each was lost to the others and unity was maintained only by accident. The value judgments implied in 'emotional nationalism' became the only unifying and guiding principle of political economy as a whole.

The whole development, ending with 'the passing of political economy' in his own time, was, in Innis' estimation, coming to an end under the pressures of an unbalanced growth of democracy. The tyranny of popular opinion and 'the political spirit' with its extremely short time horizons opened the way for the exploitation of political economy by special interests; and what the special interests wanted to use was the persuasive prestige of science when presented in mathematical and statistical form. Consequently the mathematical procedure, despite the fact that it was suitable only for the merely rational calculation of the money measure of things, became the apparent procedure of any social science that could make a show of using it. In order to make such a show, however, it was necessary to impute the logically closed, timeless continuity of abstracted quantification to the open, discontinuous processes of technological and cultural change. As social science turned to this combination of 'the mathematical and biological fallacies,' the fact that 'civilization is an art,' that 'civilization is an organization of values,' was overlooked. Loss of an awareness of the role of values meant the loss of concepts of persuasion and tolerance. Coercion became the mainstay of social organization and social science was enlisted to serve it. In short, the advance of democracy had establishd a form of national capitalism that accentuated the role of power rather than liberty and enslaved the social sciences in the service of its bureaucracies. 'We are faced,' Innis said, 'with the prospects of a new Dark Ages.'[11]

He became very pessimistic in his assessment of contemporary trends but never to such an extent that he no longer thought it worthwhile to complain. His one persistent hope seemed to be that the university would be able to rehabilitate fallen civilization.[12] He thought the university should have been immune to the rapid advance in communications techniques that had brought about an excessive and unstable growth in democratic institutions. While the sensationalist press tended to keep the public in a state of crises and fear over day to day events, the university was supposed to redress the balance with a calmer, more far-sighted opinion. Unfortunately the facts of the matter were not that way. From Innis' vantage point the history of the university seemed hardly different from the history of political economy. Caught up in the spirit of politics, like every other institution, it tended to adopt the short-view, journalistic mentality.

During the nineteenth century the university had escaped the control of crown and church by emphasizing science and mathematics, but this had meant loss of its own basic concern with the humanities. Thus, without direction, it began again to take leads from special interests; business interests, political parties, and ecclesiastical institutions. State universities multiplied and showed a particular sensitivity to political pressure. Bombarded by the competition of modern media of communication, and sorely in need of money to keep up with the rapid advance, academic communities were forced to turn their hands to popularization in return for financial contributions from special interests. As he put it, 'We need a study of the professsor as sandwichman.' In Canada in particular the universities felt the distintegrating pressures of 'colonialism, imperialism, ecclesiasticism, academic nepotism, political

11 Innis, 'Political Economy in the Modern State,' in *Political Economy in the Modern State* (1946), 138.
12 The following is taken from Innis' essays, 'The Problems of Rehabilitation,' 'The University in the Modern Crisis,' and 'A Plea for the University Tradition,' all of which are in *Political Economy and the Modern State* (1946), and from 'Some English Canadian University Problems' (1943).

affiliations and the demands of special groups.' The mid-twentieth century was witnessing 'the systematic rape of scholarship.'

Evidently, in the long run, the emancipation of the university from church and state had not been successsful and under their continuing influence it served to keep the common man down.[13] In a relatively underdeveloped country like Canada the low status of scholarship made it necessary for the universities to rely on British and American funds and personnel with the result that keeping the common man down meant subordinating native-born Canadians to the more prestigeous foreign born; for example, the transferring to Canada of an élite of British, intellectual, socialists who established a new style of politics that Innis called 'labour imperialism.' The strategy in that case was to work up sentiment in favour of government intervention and then to accept positions in Ottawa to carry it out.

With all its weaknesses the university remained Innis' hope for the future.

It is to be expected that you will ask for cures and for some improvement from the state of chaos and strife in which we find ourselves in this century. There is no cure except the appeal to reason and an emphasis on long run considerations – on the future and on the past. By a determined effort to widen our perspective we may be able to stem the currents of the moment. And in all of this such institutions as the university must be expected to play a major part ... Throughout its history the university has always exercized a moderating influence. When the terrors of the Inquisition swept across Europe it was the University of Paris which held the centralizing power of the Church, even the awful power of the Papacy, in check. In turn it has been compelled to face the threat of nationalism. While its task was enormously simplified by commercialism and capitalism these have become subordinated to the state

13 J.T. Muckle sat with Innis on the train returning to Toronto after Innis
    had delivered his presidential address to the Royal Society in 1947. When
    the conversation turned to the subject of the address Innis told Muckle
    that its theme had been that church and state had always combined in
    Canada to keep the common man down. Muckle, a Catholic priest,
    disagreed with Innis and the two decided to talk the matter over later.
    Years later Muckle told me that the second conversation had never taken
    place and that anyway Innis was right.

and the nation and have increased its difficulties in the twentieth century.
Militarism has ever been the expression of organized power and the
enemy of freedom has again accentuated its burdens. But always the
university must foster the search for truth and in its search must always
question the pretentions of organized power whether in the hands of
church or state. It will always favour the existence of a number of
centralized powers in the hope that no one of them will predominate
and exert its will and that individual freedom will have a greater chance
to survive. It will always insist that any group which pretends to have
found the truth is a fraud against civilization and that it is the search for
truth and not truth which keeps civilization alive.[14]

Innis made some attempt at a special study of the role of coercion
in the advance of civilization even though he raised the question
late and was in part distracted by his interest in the effects of
changing technology on communications. The few articles he did
write on the subject are only suggestive of what could be done.
Further, he did not make the aggressive attack on the subject that
characterized much of his other work. In large measure he simply
re-wrote his economic history bringing out the role of force. A
comparison of the texts of 'The Political Implications of Unused
Capacity'[15] and 'Unused Capacity as a Factor in Canadian Economic History,'[16] for example, suggests that he wrote the one with
the other open in front of him. Three other articles, written as a
trilogy on the subject, were of the same general character.[17] Nonetheless, some principles and conclusions emerge clearly enough.

He repeatedly used the idea that on continental land masses,
where territory can more easily be seized and held by force, politics
tends to dominate economics and the size of the political unit is
a derivative of the relative efficiencies of means of offence and
defence. European feudalism emphasized the principle of coercion.

14 Innis, 'The Canadian Situation,' an unpublished address, 8–9.
15 *Political Economy in the Modern State* (1946), 218–27.
16 1936.
17 'Imperfect Regional Competition and Political Institutions on the
    Atlantic Seaboard' (1942); 'Decentralization and Democracy' (1943);
    and 'Foreword' to M.G. Lawson, *Fur: A Study in English Mercantilism*
    (1943). Another similar essay was the 'Foreword' to K.E. Knorr,
    British Colonial Theories: 1570-1850 (1944).

During the mercantilist period, when maritime empires were built up, coercion declined and the principle of exchange became more important in the institutionalization of activity; and it was not until civilization passed from the north Atlantic to continental America that the importance and usefulness of the old feudal forms again became evident in North American federal constitutions. In this last regard Innis saw a basic difference between the politics of the United States and that of Canada. He thought that land and feudal institutions were of prime importance in American federalism, whereas the sea and commercial institutions were of prime importance in Canadian federalism. For evidence, he cited the fact that the founding fathers of the United States rejected the idea of a supreme parliament in favour of common law principles developed in the feudal period. The fathers of confederation in Canada accepted parliamentary supremacy. The American colonies laid their claims against parliament on the basis of feudal land grants from the crown. Parliament and the Canadians were concerned with commerce. By implication, the principle of coercion was more important in the United States than in Canada.

Either principle, coercion or exchange, could be used to centralize an area, but there were clear differences. Feudal institutions based on coercion were characterized by a decentralized system of exchanges so that centralization in continental areas tended to be a function of the efficiency of the use of force. Conversely, commercial institutions based on exchange were characterized by decentralized politics so that centralization in maritime areas tended to be a function of the efficiency of the price system. On these grounds Innis asserted that the emergence of centralized, but federal, democratic political institutions implied some sort of balance between the two principles of coercion and exchange. In the United States the original decentralized federalism resulted from a balance between the economic decentralization of feudal land rights and the economic centralization of commercialism in New England. The originally centralized Canadian federation was a commercial union achieved through the establishment of institutions which improved the efficiency of the price system in face of financial weaknesses in the constituent feudal colonies. By the turn of the twentieth century, however, continental centralization in North America was effecting a re-feudalization of the Canadian commercial union as provincial governments gained in strength over the federal government on the basis of control over land and resources.

From these remarks it is probably clear that Innis did not effectively raise the question of the role of coercion in economic growth. By the time he had reached this stage in the logical development of his position his concern with economic theory as such was weakening. The broader concept of the rise and fall of civilizations attracted him more. But this too may have been a logical result of his conceptualization of the elements of social action. Once force and values are accorded an independent and dynamic role a strictly economic theory of growth becomes a logical impossibility. In fact even a political theory of growth becomes a logical impossibility, for coercion is as irrelevant to the level of wealth as is the relative scarcity of goods, and for the same reasons. It is not exchange or force that determines wealth, but the way in which these two things are organized. It is the technical sophistication and the value judgments of a society which set the limit to its growth and lead it to more or less exploit this limit. In short, it is the interaction of technology and values that makes the difference in growth or decline. This Innis undertook to explore in his history of communications.

8

Values in
the nature and history
of civilization

The significance of Innis' studies of communications cannot be found in their conclusions nor in the application of those conclusions to the theory of growth, though they are interesting enough on those counts. What is significant is that Innis pursued them after long consideration of the process of economic advance, finding therein the critical problem area of economic science and leaving it to some extent explored. He emerged from an evaluation of economics with his attention riveted on the problem of values, as he put it, with 'a personal interest in public opinion – particularly the existence of broad plateaus of public opinion and the sharp breaks which occur in it from time to time – a sort of psychological or cultural approach.[1]

The subject required unusual discipline if objectivity was to be maintained (presuming it could be maintained), and Innis was acutely aware of this problem, but in the end he did not rise above his own values and, as a result, his writing took on a pessimistic tone. Which is not to deny that it was full of ironic humour, all pointing in one direction. He was half serious when he said that 'a social scientist in Canada can only survive by virtue of a sense of humour.' Some evidence of the roots of his concern can be found

1 Letter from H.A. Innis to A.H. Cole (April 2, 1943).

in his comments at the eighth meeting of the Values Discussion
Group at the University of Toronto in 1949.[2]

New techniques upset the old and leave no means of controlling them.
This is illustrated by the introduction of bombing into modern warfare.
There are no laws to control such innovations ...

The breakdown of values belongs to these inventive periods, especially
those productive of instruments of war but also those producing innovations in systems of communications such as the fast press, telegraph,
etc.

The beginning of printing is associated with a tendency to decentralization, the emphasis was on nationalism and the vernacular in language
... This is illustrated by the story of the press in the United States where
it is subsidized by the Bill of Rights which in guaranteeing the freedom
of the press actually provides the press with a guarantee of monopoly.
Powerful urban newspapers have been concerned with the control of
space (i.e. domination of a particular region) and also with domination
of time (they can release information when they choose) ... under the
guise of democracy freedom of the press has led to the defence of
monopoly.

In its broadest application, his main point was that the technicalities
of communication are a significant factor in those organizations of
values that constitute civilizations. In periods of rapid technical
advance, therefore, civilization disintegrates in confusion with atten-
dant moral and material chaos.

Innis did not have what commonly passes for a philosophic mind,
nor was he skilled in the philosopher's tools. In consequence he
failed to distinguish between ultimate values and those institutional
arrangements such as freedom of the press and universal suffrage
by which an attempt is made to realize ultimate values. But scepti-

2 The group included S.D. Clark, D. Creighton, W.T. Easterbrook,
  K. Helleiner, H.M. McLuhan, and others representing a cross-section
  of disciplines. The discussions were recorded and mimeographed for
  private circulation. Further examples of Innis' thinking in this regard
  can be found in his remarks reported in the *Proceedings of the Conference
  on the Social Sciences in the Liberal Arts College* (Princeton, April 20–2,
  1945.

cism in regard to established philosophical thought left him free to include in the category of values economic concepts of commodity and time preference and the general climate of opinion in so far as it affects particular forms of enterprise and government. This in turn coincided with his presumption that while values were radically indeterminate they were generally formulated and accepted in line with constraints and liberties occurring entirely within the context of the social process, particularly as shaped by the dominant means of communication.

Research for the communications studies was first directed to a history of the paper and printing industries. By 1945 it had matured in manuscript into a general history of communication techniques as a factor in cultural and political change.[3] From that work, which has remained unpublished, he drew the substance of the addresses and articles that *were* published between 1945 and 1952.[4] These essays condensed the factual data contained in the manuscript and made its interpretive insights more explicit. Clearly the substance of Innis' thought was embodied in the published work. The following analysis and précis, therefore, has been based on the latter.

Given the tremendous historical range of the study, 4241 BC to 1950 AD, use of primary documents was impossible, perhaps unnecessary. In fact, even the secondary sources were mined rather than assimilated. Innis knew precisely what he was looking for. At one time he wrote to Arthur Cole that Gibbon's *Decline and Fall* was written in relation to a view of the British Empire.[5] His own history of communications was written with a view to clarifying the character of the mid-twentieth century. The ancient world was a laboratory in which he asked his questions and tested his hypotheses.

In the Innisian scheme of things civilization is the organization of values. His questions, therefore, pertained to the determinants of

3 Innis, '*A History of Communications*' (microfilm).
4 With the exception of 'The English Press in the Nineteenth Century' (1945), and 'The Newspaper in Economic Development' (1942). The essays were published in three volumes: *Empire and Communications* (1950), *The Bias of Communication* (1951), and *Changing Concepts of Time* (1952).
5 Letter from Innis to A.H. Cole (March 26, 1951).

the values involved in any given case. What were the conditions under which the priorities of public opinion changed, or failed to change, and how were economic and political institutions organized in relation to the change in values? How do these institutions face up to the demands of time and space? That is, with a given set of technical constraints, how do economic and political institutions organize to cope with the fact of existence in space and time? To what extent does a civilization appreciate the difficulties of survival through time, and in what way does it combine elements of continuity and change as it addresses itself to the problem? To what extent does it extend itself in space, and in what way does it combine elements of uniformity and diversity within its boundaries? From the point of view of the building up of a civilization, what are the strengths and weaknesses of the ways in which survival and extension are achieved? How does the consequent bias towards extension or survival affect the possibility of a reorganization of values? He did not, however, ask the one question that would have taken him directly back to the starting point of his research; at least, he did not make it the focal point of his interest. That question is, how does the value bias of any civilization become incorporated into the economic process of capital deepening or widening? Perhaps the answer to that question was too obvious for mention.

It would be entirely misleading to attempt to draw a consistent set of answers from the communications essays. In the first place Innis' approach was exploratory and consequently involved no point of final logical closure. In the second, the published articles were prepared for oral presentation to a variety of audiences in Britain, the United States, and Canada. They were never intended to constitute a comprehensive doctrine. This is not to say that nothing at all of a generally applicable nature can be drawn from them. But that what follows here is merely an interpretive discussion of salient points.[6]

6 In point of fact the essays are extremely repetitious in regard to factual data and most of them are explorations, in one way or another, of a limited set of ideas. This facilitates a discussion of salient points and obviates the need for extensive citations and references. A few articles can be taken as a fair representation of the lot: 'The Newspaper in Economic Development' (1942); 'The Oral Tradition in Greek

As a first step the Innisian sense of the phrase 'the bias of communication' must be clarified. Its basic significance in the essays is
the relative efficiency of the media used to transfer information over
space and through time. Usually the phrase appears in the context
of engineering rather than economic efficiency. For example, information preserved in some form of writing is more efficiently transferred through time, but if it is written on stone rather than (say)
paper it is less efficiently transferred over space. In consequence of
some such simple relative efficiency in its dominant means of communication, a civilization will tend to have duration or extension as
the case may be. Of course the essays treat the actual achievement of
duration or extension as a more complex process than this. Relative
efficiency in one respect may imply relative inefficiency in another.
For instance, a civilization endowed with written records has solved
the problem of merely transferring information through time, but it
is then left with the problem of coping with the accumulation of
information as time passes. It will have to develop some technique
for processing ever larger quantities of information. In the absence
of offsetting factors it may resort to a categorization of information
for treatment by specialists, but this would be destructive of social
unity. Alternatively it may reduce the problem of quantity by merely
copying the past rather than acquiring new information. Thus Innis
explored the possibility that division, dogmatism, social rigidity, and
want of originality constitute the problem of duration (time) that
accompanies the spread of writing. The weakness of a bias in favour
of duration could be a low level of internal cohesion and/or the
dissipation of energy in mere survival.

If a durable medium for writing is particularly transportable a
different set of problems may arise. Transportable media facilitate
political organization over wide geographic areas. Extension in
space and centralization are symptomatic of the bias of writing taken
from this point of view. In such a case easy spatial extension of
administration could conflict with regional institutions supported by

Civilization,' in *Empire and Communications* (1950); 'Minerva's Owl,'
and 'The Bias of Communication' in *The Bias of Communication* (1951);
and 'The Strategy of Culture' in *Changing Concepts of Time* (1952).
The discussion here, however, is not confined to the material in these
five articles.

other media with a bias in favour of duration. In the absence of restraining factors the simplest means to resolve the resulting tensions would be centrally organized force. In many of the essays Innis explored the possibility that the weakness of the spatial bias is impatience wtih time-consuming solutions, a tendency to use coercion and, consequently, to dissipate energy in military activity.

It seems clear enough on Innis' own showing that the strengths of one medium may not offset the weaknesses of another. Certainly he never elaborated the logic of an argument to show the closed complementarity of two media. Nonetheless, he continually presented the idea of some sort of balance of biases. His treatment of the relationship between religion and politics (church and state) is unintelligible without reference to such a concept. He generally presumed that the state as an instiution was heavily committed to some medium with a spatial bias. Thus the state and its politics were associated with present-mindedness, spatial extension, and the use of force. Against this the church as an institution was presumed to rely on a medium with a relative efficiency through time. The church and its presence was associated with longer time horizons and thought control rather than force. On the basis of an assumed complementarity of biases an alliance between church and state was treated by Innis as a powerful factor in imperial success.

The Byzantine empire developed on the basis of a compromise between organizations reflecting the bias of different media: that of papyrus in the development of an imperial bureaucracy in relation to a vast area and that of parchment in the development of an ecclesiastical hierarchy in relation to time. It persisted with a success parallelled by that of the compromise between monarchial elements based on stone and religious elements based on clay which characterized the long period of the Kassite dynasty in the Babylonia empire.[7]

A statement such as this immediately suggests to the reader questions of measurement in regard to the relative durability and transportability of parchment and papyrus and of stone and clay. Beyond this there is the further question of measuring the significance of any

7 *Empire and Communications* (1950), 139.

relative efficiency that may be found to exist. But Innis himself did not try to explain everything in terms of the merely technical co-efficients implied by the discussion here. At critical points in his argument he introduced other factors in the historical process: geographic controls, technical advance in weaponry, the relative scarcity of resources, the persistence of institutions despite technical change, free choice. All of these find their place in the sequence of events. Given Innis' presumptions about the role of values and their radical indeterminacy it would have been inconsistent of him to accord media bias anything but a limiting or permissive role. In fact he did not push his argument beyond this point, but because he felt that an important factor was being completely neglected by others he attached great and well defined significance to it.

In the Innisian usage, as already suggested, media bias implies more than simple extension or duration for the social system in question. It implies a distinctive set of institutions with a related set of values and the sort of conceptualization of reality that a particular set of values in its turn implies. For example, whether relatively transportable or not, written communications excel in durability and thus may engender a conservative character in thought. Oral communication may encourage an innovating character of thought by reason of the scope for individual contribution where there is no exact, voluminous reproduction. Innis repeatedly returned to the idea that the creativity of an oral tradition could be a factor in solving problems of conservatism built up in relation to writing. He was suggesting a balance or compromise between two concepts of time. In a civilization communicating by means of the eye (e.g. writing, architecture) time is appreciated and institutionalized in a peculiar way. In a civilization communicating by means of the ear (e.g. the spoken word, radio) it is all different. Time in the first instance will be conceptualized as linear, that is having a recorded beginning and a continuity, and sometimes a prophesied and recorded end. In the second instance it will be cyclical, involving a sequence of different times, each being a renewal of time. Innis explored the possibility that flexibility consequent upon scope for initiative in aural time could counterbalance the rigidities implied by visual time.

The Innisian concept of balance does not imply harmony. It is the balance of competition or countervailing power. Its opposite is monopoly. But the idea of monopoly is not simple in Innis' work since it is used in at least two principle ways without specific definition in either case.

There are points in the essays at which the term monopoly clearly signifies the traditional idea of a form of enterprise deviating for technical or proprietorial reasons from the model of perfect competition as commonly conceived. In Innis' broad use this signification could apply to anything from imperfect competition to perfect monopoly, and could refer to the control of scarce commodities, skills, political influence, or information. A second way in which Innis uses the term is not unrelated to the first but differs from it in the way in which a macro concept differs from a micro concept in economic theory. This macro concept of monopoly signifies the dominance of one medium of communication in a social system. In such a case the firms and industries involved may be perfectly competitive but the medium itself as the dominant channel of intercourse monopolizes information and, in consequence, the general climate of opinion, with the effect that one civilization (organization of values) and its vested interests are entrenched. It was not unusual for him to imply interdependence between the two kinds of monopoly but since he did not at any point elaborate the connection it is perhaps best to leave the matter at the present point.

Taking it in either meaning Innis' judgment on unrestricted monopoly was the traditional one – that it smothers the vitality necessary for processes of growth. The advantages derived by the vested interests of the monopoly invite competition from without, while the one sidedness associated with it exaggerates and perpetuates weaknesses that can be exploited by the outsiders. In addition, the conservative bias of entrenched vested interests prevents innovating energy from making significant contact with the basic formality of the system. In an extreme case the alternatives become invasion from without, revolution from within, or stagnation. Starting from this point of view on monopoly, Innis elaborated some possible types or patterns of cultural development associated with the spread and evolution of visual media of communication. Collectively the patterns may be referred to as the *Minerva's owl effect*. He himself did not use precisely this term but he did use 'the flight of Minerva's owl' as a metaphor to describe the phenomena in question. The Minerva's owl effect takes three related forms in the essays, though Innis made no attempt to give them clear definition or to relate them to one another.

The first form depicts the way in which a culture will reach a peak of vitality and productiveness at precisely that moment at which it is about to succumb to an alien culture. This is explained in at least two ways. The first way postulates that both the old and the new civilizations are characterized by stultifying monopolies, so that a burst of original work and the formation of classics in art and literature takes place during the brief period in which the one system more or less balances the other. The second way treats the phenomenon as a characteristic of the general frontier of visual communications systems. Beyond the influence of monopolies related to visual media there exists a variety of oral traditions. As visual communication extends itself it picks up the content of these traditions and formalizes it into classics which then are more or less slavishly copied as the vitality of the oral tradition is suffocated in the relatively conservative world of writing and print.

The second and third forms of the Minerva's owl effect are variations of the first. The second signifies the fact that cultural flowering does not take place in the same place or in the same way twice. This is taken to be a consequence of the conservative character of a written tradition which, by means of its classical productions in any field of learning or the arts, stifles the creativity of the traditions from which they were drawn, and indeed of any tradition into which they are injected. The stifling effect of the classics forces creativity to move in entirely new directions if it leaves room for movement at all. The third form, that most frequently referred to by Innis, illustrates well the simple proposition underlying the Minerva's owl effect. It signifies the fact that innovations generally take place in the fringe areas of monopolized systems. In other words, where there is liberty there is creativity; and the absence of liberty is not so much a consequence of force as of the intellectual and moral assumptions inherent in the bias of the means of communication.

All of this had direct implications in regard to the critical character of the social sciences and the general problem of values; for, on this showing, every civilization, being a biased organization of values, is incapable of objectively assessing its own position. From this there follow two clear propostions. First, scientific objectivity is impossible in social studies. That is to say it is impossible for men whose minds are structured by the bias of one system of communications to take an objective view either of their own culture or of cultures formed under the influence of other systems of communications. Second, values are the significant content of presumed objective economic and political data so that the subject matter itself of the social sciences is non-objective and therefore indeterminate.

Innis most clearly made this second point in relation to the way in which the communications industries create markets for themselves. This is the case in which advertisers advertise advertising. Innis pointed out that just as the common commercial variety of advertisement creates values in the form of commodity and time preferences, so publishing in general is a form of advertising in which values of almost every sort are created and institutionalized. In short, publishers advertise a climate of opinion in which they have a vested interest, for the more prevalent the sort of values they sell the larger the market for selling them. They are the agents of acculturation associated with some particular values, and naturally they are reluctant to leave room for competitive interests using modern devices to propagate new ones. But it is all more serious than their intentions. If publishers are involved in establishing and institutionalizing values, then what they sell is not a commodity like others. It is not a commodity sold in the market, but is the very foundation of the market itself. In this sense the communications industry carries itself by its own boot straps, because it creates its own space and time – its own closed, self-sustaining world.

The closed circularity of this situation is even more complex than indicated so far. Innis pointed out that every competitive seller in the information market will make some attempt to meet demand by tailoring output to what people want prior to any advertisement. He will try both to please the public and to educate it into thinking that he is the only publisher who can. Thus the process of market creation in the case of a new medium will involve both exploitation of existing values and inculcation of those which, being peculiar to the medium, entrench its position. If one carries this matter to the basic logical proposition involved, it is that the vested interests of each medium tend to propose as right and natural that which peculiarly appears as a value within the system that the medium itself creates. The means thus dictate the ends or, as Innis put it, 'nature copies art.' And so it is with the social sciences which are also a product of the publishing industry. What begins as a bare-faced moral assertion in what is essentially a cooked-up advertising campaign soon comes to be presented as a true statement of observable, objective fact. Moreover, if people believe a statement about social behaviour they act accordingly so that the faith they have in the assertion makes it true. Nature copies art.

The attempts that Innis made to apply this sort of analysis to the economic and political problems of the twentieth century were characterized by indifferent success. The best examples of his efforts in this regard are the three essays 'The Newspaper in Economic Development,' 'Roman Law and the British Empire,' and 'The Military Implications of the American Constitution.'[8] Some discussion of these may serve to bring out both the character and the limitations of Innis' work in the communications essays.

In 'The Newspaper in Economic Development,' he attempted to rationalize two major problems of the North American economic system, increasing monopolization and periodic depression. He attributed the increase of monopolistic forms of business to the effects of advertising on market preferences and to the increase in business overhead in the form of advertising expenses in consequence of its effectiveness. Behind this phenomenon lay a complex of technical and economic changes. Advances in the technique of printing increased the overhead costs of the newspaper industry, creating a need for larger markets. Formation of larger markets for news was facilitated by the telegraph, which not only made instant, factual, national news a possibility, but created the necessary organizational underpinning for newspaper chains. In the industrial and business

8 The first of these is to be found in the *Journal of Economic History* (1942), and the other two in *Changing Concepts of Time* (1952).

sectors proportionately increasing overhead costs and rapid creation of a national market, following the advent of the telegraph and the high speed press, led to rapid formation of trusts and monopolistic enterprise in the latter part of the nineteenth century. Changes in the structure of the information industry and the new kind of news moved the press away from political patronage to reliance on commercial advertising. Thus the formation of chains of newspapers to extend the market for information was accompanied by changes in the information marketed and this, in turn, altered the market a second time. The whole character of public information changed. Bombarded with sensationalist reporting of day-to-day events, and with an increasing quantity of market news coloured by sensationalism, the time preferences of the market changed. In fact an entirely new concept of time insinuated itself into the system, and expressed itself in the form of increasingly shorter time horizons and a concomitant increase in the preference for liquidity. Major adjustments in the system had been necessary for some time when more changes accompanying the advent of radio precipitated the depression.

Innis' explanation seems plausible enough. In fact it contains extremely enlightening insights into the general process of economic change. On close examination, however, the logical structure of the thing does not hang together and what stands is only the insight. His description of how things actually worked themselves out is clearly inadequate. For example, there is a description of the shortening of time horizons under the influnce of a 'present-minded' press. At the same time there is a description of the build-up of overhead, implying a lengthening of time horizons, again under the influence of the press. One wonders how a system dominated by one medium, and presumably shaped in all respects with the bias of the medium, could develop such disharmony of parts. From another point of view it is hard to understand how all of this can be discussed under the heading of monopoly when technical change, the emergence of new media, and tumultuous competition characterize the system. Of course, one could propose perspectives and logical connections that tie all the apparently disjointed parts, but Innis did not elaborate all that.

The two political articles, 'The Military Implications of the

American Constitution' and 'Roman Law and the British Empire,' converge on the weaknesses of Innis' later work. Both deal with the implications of a written constitution in a legal system built up in relation to the spoken word. By the term 'Roman law' he meant to signify a written law embodying the concepts and conservatism of a written tradition. On the one hand he extolled the creativity of the oral tradition of English common law, on the other he condemned its present-mindedness and its emphasis on factual data. Similarly he ascribed commendable oral qualities to the present-minded press while attacking it as a monopoly in a written tradition. He deplored the rigidities of a written constitution but went on to suggest that the problems connected with it arose because the oral creativity of common law politics affected the interpretation of it. In the end he added up these and other elements in the situation to come to the conclusion that in consequence of a general want of balance and equilibrium the American system was biased in the direction of space and military expansion.

The reader is left to wonder at the strength of the moral judgment passed in the process of an apparently objective analysis. Clearly Innis was not objective. Given the obvious successes of the American system why cannot its elements be added up to constitute a constructive balance? The question may be put this way, how can one distinguish between opposing elements in disequilibrium and opposing elements in balance? There seems no way in which this can be done in the absence of gratuitous moral assertion. Certainly Innis did not do it in such a way as to provide an adequate basis for prediction. The weaknesses of Innis' later work can best be understood in the light of his own conclusions about the indeterminacy of values and their problematic role in social science.

9

The place of Innis
in the history of economics

When Innis died, the communications studies were still of a seminal character, and they had only suggestively been referred back to the problem of economic growth from which they had originated. It is difficult, therefore, to present a summary of his contribution to economics, one that would neatly capsulize his thought. In fact the only way in which this can be done to any extent is by focusing attention on the stream of economic thought against which he was reacting. There are, of course, disadvantages in this approach. Since Innis rejected price economics for its inability to handle the problem of growth, his positive contribution cannot then be made the centre of attention. It may be, however, that enough has been said on the latter count already and that something can be gained from a shift back to the point of view with which our whole account started. The summary, therefore, begins with a statement of those weaknesses in price theory from which the Innisian reconstruction began.

Quite probably none of the nineteenth-century marginalist school, the price economists, really believed that economics was a science on equal footing with the natural sciences. But at times they talked as if it was and there was a general belief that it would be a good thing if it could be reduced to a thorough-going science. On both of these counts neoclassical analysis was open to criticism, and, of course, those who did not like the sort of conclusions to which the neoclassicists came exploited the possibilities. Among the critics, perhaps the most successful, was Thorstein Veblen. Veblen not only criticized the analysis on the grounds that it was unscientific, he repudiated the whole approach as an apologetic for the instutional arrangements of an earlier and long defunct stage in industrial advance. Important questions relating to the level of physical productivity and the evolution of industrial organization, in his view, could not be properly raised within the logical framework of price economics. It was the question of growth that concerned him, and Innis' interest in growth was a continuation of that concern. The Innisian doctrine grows out of those points of weakness in neoclassical theory to which Veblen pointed.

Neoclassical economics can be taken as that body of knowledge which has commonly passed under the titles of price economics, price theory and value theory. No doubt each title has specific connotations, but the subject matter indicated by each has sufficient in common with the others to be included with them as one particular division of political economy. Within that division the discipline can be described as an attempt to elaborate a consistent means-ends conceptualization of human behaviour in terms of which prices can be rationalized as an adequate measure of both means and ends. The difficulties arise in regard to the establishment of *the adequacy of the measure*. Throughout the history of the development of the discipline, however, there has been a persistent tendency to presume that the obex to scientific conclusions would be *indeterminacy in the price*, with the result that the main intent has been to elaborate the process of determination rather than to explore the significance of the prices whether determinate or not.

Putting aside, therefore, the question of whether or not prices have been found to be determinate in empirically verifiable theory, the points of critical difficulty in the logical elaboration of the conceptualization represent those junctures at which information has to be translated from the concrete categories of engineering and the objective categories of ethics and metaphysics into the mathematical categories of relative scarcity – that is, into prices. Upon the success of the translation depends the success of economics as a social *science.*

The persistence of the difficulties involved in the translation has been most evident in the history of welfare economics. In that branch of the discipline the primitive assumption that prices measure values in some absolute sense (cardinally and additively) had to be abandoned in favour of the assumption that they measure only relatively (ordinally and with respect to quantities of other goods in comparison). At the same time there was a contraction in the extent to which the qualitative element in values was assumed to be measured by price, and the term 'utility' was replaced by the term 'satisfaction.' This tendency to abandon the attempt to translate values into prices has continued to the point at which any implication of value content has been removed from welfare economics, except for the assertion that it is better to be in a chosen position. That is to say, the assessment of value content has been reduced to a matter of vacuous choice. In some of its more recent forms the whole theory with all of its logical elaboration is virtually defined by the presumption that to have chosen is the final good.

Similar difficulties have marked the attempt to develop a scientific theory of production. Particularly, the lumpiness and general incomparability of physical inputs have prevented their meaningful translation into the language of price. In some instances the problem has been talked out of existence by the pretence that physical units can be measured in terms of 'efficiency units,' or even of price itself, without begging the basic question of what prices are supposed to measure. But even supposing there were some sense in which the translation into price could be made, the translation itself, by reducing everything to the terms of relative scarcity, would effectively eliminate any consideration of qualitative content. That is to say, the formal structure of price theory is equally applicable to any set of physical inputs regardless of their qualities or technical, quantitative effectiveness in production, for the theory has nothing at all to say about this aspect of economic behaviour.

Here is the point. The very concept of price as a measure of *relative* scarcity, logically excludes any consideration of the absolute amount of anything and therefore it excludes any consideration of the processes of growth in absolute amount. Furthermore, even in their own terms, prices cannot be assigned a definite meaning unless they are determined in established competitive markets or some other established and rationally organized institution. The implication of this is that, under the usual conditions of economic growth when engineering technique and organizational devices are in state of flux, prices are unreliable as an indication of what is happening. In short, it is in regard to those things which relate particularly to economic growth and development that the price analysis is most open to criticism, and it was in this regard that Veblen criticized the concepts and logic of neoclassical value theory with the following remark.

They are hedonistically 'natural' categories of such taxonomic force that their elemental lines of cleavage run through the facts of any given economic situation, regardless of use and wont, even where the situation does not permit these lines of cleavage to be seen by men and recognized by use and wont; so that, e.g., a gang of Aleutian Islanders slushing about in the wrack and surf with rakes and magical incantations for the capture of shell fish are held in point of taxonomic reality to be engaged on a feat of hedonistic equilibration in rent, wages and interest. Indeed for economic theory of this kind that is all there is to any economic situation.[1]

Innis accepted Veblen's critique of neoclassical economics, so much so that his work presupposes Veblen's and cannot be understood outside of that context. But Innis came on the scene a generation after Veblen, and was aware of the difficulties into which Veblen himself had fallen in his attempt to construct a truly scientific economics. The Innisian reconstruction of economic theory begins with the failure of Veblen as well as the failure of neoclassical theory.

The weaknesses of the Veblenian system are the reverse reflection of the weaknesses Veblen had pointed out in traditional value theory. As he saw it, the basic problem with price economics is the

1 Thorstein Veblen, 'Professor Clark's Economics,' in *The Place of Science in Modern Civilization* (1919; reprinted 1961), 193.

teleological character of the reasoning involved. It is a biased hedonism, a system of arguments that run entirely in terms of final causality, though they are arranged in such a way that the final cause, the values of the system, are not specified. The natural sciences, which are truly scientific in the sense acceptable to Veblen, run in terms of direct efficient cause without consideration of any goal or purpose that may be involved. Accordingly, he attempted to build a scientific economics by elaborating the effects of the non-teleological forces of blind instinct and technologically defined physical limitation. Values were dismissed from his discussion by being reduced to obsolescent behaviour patterns, the vestiges of outmoded technologies. From this it followed that any economizing in relation to such pseudo values would be a pernicious block to the advance of productivity proceeding under the stimulus of blind instinct. In other words, Veblen ostensibly solved the problem of social science by asserting that values are non-existent and that what appears as values is merely a dependent variable of technique. This, of course, every bit as much as price theory, left a vacuum where the qualitative aspects of initiative and energy (i.e. values) should have been. Like the price economists, Veblen was therefore incapable of drawing any policy implications without surreptitiously insinuating a value judgment into his argument at some unacknowledged point. He achieved this by means of his taxonomic treatment of instincts.

During Veblen's own lifetime a second, less radical attempt to remedy the weaknesses of price economics developed along narrower, more commonly partisan lines. This merely revisionist movement was destined to raise the problem of social science in an entirely different form. Charles Horton Cooley was one initiator of the stream, but the argument received its most extensive elaboration from B.M. Anderson.[2] Anderson's statement can be summed up in two points. First, there exist social values that are in some way different and separate from individual values. Second, any actual set of prices may or may not express existing individual and social values. The implication of both points is that values are, in logic and in fact, prior to prices. They constitute an independent factor in the social system which in the absence of suitable institutions will not be adequately reflected in the structure of prices.

2 B.M. Anderson, *Social Value* (Boston, 1911).

While Anderson's contention was likely to illuminate the problems of economic growth and development, the particular concerns of the nineteen-twenties and -thirties did not take the matter in that direction. Emphasis was put on the implications for optimizing behaviour in a static context. The first consideration was to elaborate the place of social values in price economics and to take steps to see that a suitable representative of the social conscience be given some authority over the structure of prices in the real world. But this meant that if the idea of scientific economics was to be maintained there would have to be some sort of scientific ethic to set the values of social conscience. Thus the revisionists were on the way to a social science based on static teleological presumptions quite opposed to the Veblenian scheme.

It was at this point, however, in the ramification of these ideas into public academic discussion that the problem of social science began to intrude itself into the focus of Innis' attention. In 1917, when Innis was in his first year at the University of Chicago, Anderson expounded his doctrine of social value before a group of young economists who had come together at the meetings of the American Economic Association to discuss the reconstruction of economic theory. Two of these men, A.B. Wolfe and R.G. Tugwell, accepted the idea of social value and then asserted the possibility of scientific ethics, thus preserving the possibility of a scientific economics. Two others, J.M. Clark and F.H. Knight, both of whom were admirers of Veblen and teachers of Innis, accepted the critical work of both Veblen and Anderson but refused to accept either the instinct hypothesis of the one or the scientific ethics hypothesis that had come to be associated with the other. In other words they abandoned the possibility of a scientific economics.

A debate ensued between the proponents of the two views, lasting well into the nineteen-thirties if not beyond. It was during the course of one particular round in this debate in 1934 that Innis and E.J. Urwick became publicly involved with the issue. In fact, the dispute had enjoyed a subliminal existence in academic gossip and departmental seminars in Canada for some time before 1935, with the result that when the opposing arguments were drawn up in print they were by no means a mirror reflection of positions held in the United States.

In the late nineteen-twenties, after Urwick had become head of the department of political economy at Toronto, Innis read a paper on the fur trade at a departmental meeting. He had just published his Veblen bibliography and, quite likely, the paper and the ensuing discussion showed him to be moving along distinctly Veblenian lines. Urwick, however, had just published his book, *The Social Good,* in which he took a distinctly non-Veblenian approach. Naturally he reacted to Innis by taking *something like* what has here been called the revisionist position. Urwick believed that with a consensus serving as a social conscience political adjustments should be made to affect the structure of prices. To Innis' mind this simply opened the door to political activity on the part of economists, putting them as interested parties into a situation that they were supposed to observe with objectivity. Against this eventuality he insisted that some room be left for the scientific objectivity to which Veblen had aspired. As economics became more openly a partisan activity, however, it became increasingly difficult to find any grounds for objectivity in it. Innis was forced back to a point where he was outside economics itself, trying to judge the objective significance of bias within it. He included the economist-politician among the phenomena to be studied in a scientific approach to economics. To the extent that the value judgments of biased economics could be shown to be determinate and persistent the Veblenian concept of social science could be retained. This was the beginning of the communications studies.

Despite the enthusiasm with which he held his opinions, a number of distractions prevented Innis from launching a full scale project until the summer of 1940. For a few years, therefore, his concept of social science remained vague and incomplete. Although he had accepted Veblen's general approach he had rejected both the theory of instincts and its corollary that society would be better off if the engineer were liberated from the constraints of the price system. Thus, having divested Veblen's system of the means by which the problem of values had been covered over he would have to find some other way of dealing with it.

After 1936 the department of political economy at Toronto made a determined effort to build up a staff in the field of sociology.

Expansion had begun under Urwick, but Innis himself was in charge when the sociologists clarified their position in regard to the nature of social science. The matter broke in 1940 in a flurry of debate over whether or not sociology was legitimately a branch of social science. The sociologists, of course, took the stand that it was and tried to prove their point by insisting on a deterministic approach. In one sense Innis' reaction was surprising. Considering his own difficulties with Urwick some ten years earlier, one would have expected him to be sympathetic with a scientific and deterministic point of view. This was not the case. The events of the intervening years had changed the emphasis in his own mind. Rapid growth of collectivization and nationalization at the end of the depression ran strongly against his own individualism and seemed the more insidious for being justified in the name of economic science. In Germany, the deterministic approach was exploited in the form of geo-politics to provide pseudo-scientific rationalization for military expansion. In face of this Innis began to appreciate the wisdom of insisting that scientific social science in any form was an impossibility. Thus the arrival of scientific sociology at Toronto precipitated Innis' final judgment on the question of social science. He brought his conceptualization of the social system to a point of logical closure by asserting the existence and radical importance of an independent and indeterminate principle of initiative in human behaviour. Thus he replaced Veblen's theory of instincts with a theory of the creativity of the individual and from this it followed that a truly scientific economics was impossible.

Having settled the main issue in this way, the next logical step was to work out the implications of his assertion as they appeared in the relationship of values to prices and particularly to the processes of growth or decline. Here again the demands of logic were supported by circumstances. When, in 1939, the Imperial Oil Company requested that a course in merchandising be offered by the School of Commerce, Innis found himself involved in the economics of advertising. Now, it is the function of advertising to create the commodity and time preferences that enter into market price. The economics of advertising, therefore, is exactly the same thing as the analysis of the economist-politician, for both deal with the determinants of the value infrastructure of prices. Quite logically he combined advertising and politics to form one problem area in economics. Its question was, in what way and to what extent are market preferences, political and religious beliefs and, in fact, the whole climate of opinion determined in regard to the values involved. This was the basic question of the communications essays.

In answering this question Innis continued to take the Veblenian approach, but only up to a point. His belief in the existence of creativity as a factor in economic change eliminated any pretense of deterministic science. Within the world of each medium of communication, means determined ends and values of a relative sort were in large measure determined; but the emergence of new media and new values was determined only to the limited extent to which the political power of vested interests could prevent change. As Innis' analysis passed from one world of values to another, only one element with independent and ultimate significance remained constant – the creativity of the inidividual. Putting this in terms of the problem of social science as set out earlier, not only is it impossible to translate values into prices but, even if the translation were made, prices could not be determinate. Values in themselves are indeterminate and therefore of such a shifting and indefinable character as to be essentially unfit as a subject for scientific investigation.

The whole development from the inception of neoclassical theory to H.A. Innis is reminiscent of the parable of the man from whom the devil was cast out. The devil wandered for a while in dry places and then he returned, bringing with him seven other devils worse than himself. Innis did manage to retain one ultimate, independent value in his system, the creativity of the individual. Translating this into the categories of modern welfare economics it means 'to have chosen is good.' In welfare economics, however, the choice is vacuous and static, whereas Innis' creativity implies all the crude productivity, the destructive power, and the dynamism of the restless human spirit.

10

The place of Innis
in Canadian economics

Harold Innis wrote at the very end of a period of rapid expansion in which, by means of the railroad and the telegraph, continental economies came into existence, flourished, and then regressed into depression and war. It was the end of that era for all western civilization in which political economy was widely believed to explain some natural order with which it was inopportune if not disastrous for governments to interfere. In Canada, a marginal area in which *laissez-faire* had been only a theory, the end of general expansion meant the end of the National Policy of 1878. Thus Innis found himself with a double task; first to devise a political economy suited to the Canadian case, and then to put it to use. He faced the same problem as men like Robert Gourlay and John Rae who had come at the beginning of the era. They were forced to abandon accepted dogmas in order to construct the theoretical basis for national development in a hinterland economy. They worked with foresight, and he with hindsight, but it was the same task, and the same sort of economics emerged. Innis has his place secured with those who have been ready to transcend the preconceptions of metropolitan social science to work for the general advance of Canada.

The success of Innis' doctrine in the period following his own has not been evidently spectacular, except in so far as it has been reflected in the popular works of Marshall McLuhan. While the importance of W.T. Easterbrook and people around him at Toronto testifies to Innis' lasting impression, they have not constituted a school with a distinctive theoretical or political position. In some measure this may be accounted for by the character of Innisian theory. Historical theories of growth tend to focus on the past with little attempt to assess, in their own context, the technical constraints and social goals of the future. Given Innis' historical situation, it is understandable that this tendency was accentuated in his case. In fact it has not been until quite recently that new constraints, problems and alternatives have become evident. Along with this has come a mild revival of interest in his work, but it has not involved any hope of finding therein an immediate resolution of the present impasse. In so far as the situation is new, history has nothing to say about it.

Marshall McLuhan has only been interested in a portion of the Innisian reconstruction, and it would be wrong to presume that he has tried to do what Innis did. Certainly he has not been trying to complete Innis' unfinished work, as some at one time alleged. The elaboration of the difference, however, involves some close if not tedious reasoning and requires more than a little space. The present discussion of Innis' influence, therefore, can best be divided into two main parts, the first dealing with the progress of economics in Canada in the post-Innisian era, and the second an analysis of the work of Marshall McLuhan.

By the end of the Innisian era it was generally agreed that the entire question of Canadian economic development could best be handled in terms of 'the staples thesis,' Just what that meant, however, what staples thesis or whose staples thesis, was very much in doubt. Was it the mere development of staple exports that constituted progress, or was there something more? If there was something more, what was it and how was it related to the export base? Innis' contribution had been, in fact, an explanation of the relationship between staple exports, the National Policy of 1878, and the consequent growth and structure of the Canadian economy; but there were some elements in the process which, in consequence of his apologetic approach, he did not clearly see. In the immediate post-war period these elements conspired to reduce the perceived importance of the staples approach.

Aggressive participation of domestic governments in the growth and development of British North America began about 1820 with support from the theories of Robert Gourlay, Joseph Bouchette, and John Rae in the Canadas and of John Young, T.C. Haliburton, and Abraham Gesner in the Maritimes. None of these theorists suggested that the mere exploitation of staples constituted development. In fact all suggested either the use of staple exports as a means to development or the reduction of the staple trades altogether. Differences among them followed from their varying degrees of economic sophistication and their chosen instruments of policy. A list of the latter would include the tariff, taxes on improved and unimproved land, the sale of crown lands to settlers, an issue of paper money, subsidies, technical improvements in agricultural methods, and imperial loans for the improvement of transportation. Besides these nationalistic theorists there was a free trade interest in the Maritimes early in the century and, by the eighteen-forties, in the Canadas. Thus, corresponding to a broad categorization of positions, there were three main interest groups competing for control of national policy prior to 1878: a free trade group favouring an open economy based on staple exports, a group favouring balanced, independent growth through the creation of appropriate monetary institutions, and a group favouring balanced growth through harnessing the credit potential of staple exports. It was the compromise position of the last group that won the day in 1878, and it was that policy and its consequences that Innis reconstructed.

According to Innis the National Policy was a clear case of creating governmental institutions to achieve balanced growth through the use of staple exports. Thus the development in western Canada of a wheat staple for export was directly connected with protection for manufacturers in central Canada. In the beginning, capital was borrowed with government guarantees on the basis of a surplus developing in the staple export sector. The borrowed capital was used to build the necessary technical infra-structure in the West and was retired, in large measure, through revenue from the tariff.

At the same time the tariff created a protected market that enabled domestic industry to grow on a surplus transferred from the staples producing sectors. The West was born, and central Canada developed metropolitan characteristics. The Maritimes had, in part, expected to share in the build-up of manufacturing. In the end they lost their position to the West and to central Canada.

So it was that free trade exponents and soft money people were put in the opposition and a problem of regional disparities was initiated. Most of the disaffected gathered in the Liberal party only to be disappointed again, and continuation of the National Policy by the Liberals after 1896 became a major factor in the rise of third parties. Soft money advocates eventually received expression in the Social Credit party; the Progressives sponsored free trade and anticombines legislation; and the separatist tendencies of regionally based parties became an ever present threat to confederation. In short, the first half of twentieth century Canada had arrived. The second half was in its period of gestation; as tight money policies and the tariff created a situation in which growth took place through the entrance of foreign equity capital in the form of branch plants. Thus the centralization of North America under the aegis of the multi-national coroporation was facilitated and the problems of decentralization in Canada were aggravated.

When most of these problems reached crisis proportions in the 'twenties and 'thirties, Innis appeared as an apologist for the policy of 1878, a champion of one-Canada theories, and an incipient opponent of American penetration. But the depression lingered on until it became clearly evident that the old national policy had run its course and its supporters had nothing new to offer. By the nineteen-fifties Innis and those who would have seen the matter as he did were swamped by both the soft money Keynesian group and the continentalist free traders.

Immediately after the war Keynesian compensatory finance was adopted in Canada as a new nationl policy, but it proved to be ill suited to regionally diverse and open economy such as the Canadian. Long-run problems of a 'structural' nature related to growth cannot be handled by stabilization policy alone. The force of these problems broke into the open at the time of the Coyne and Gordon controversies between 1957 and 1963, and crystallized eventually in the form of a department of regional economic expansion. Evidently long-run factors that had preoccupied Innis were again making themselves felt and the consequent renewed search for a national policy led to a revival of interest in his work. It can hardly be said, however, that he had again risen to the position of foremost exponent of Canadian economics.

In many ways formation of national policy in the mid-twentieth century parallelled that of the mid-nineteenth. The key dates are 1847 and 1957. In both years Canada was faced with suddenly curtailed markets in Europe. Immediately, in both instances, a free trade group established itself in Montreal and began pamphleting for a national policy of commercial liberty. In the earlier instance reciprocity was achieved within seven years while nationalist tendencies showed themselves only gradually, issuing first in the tariff of 1858 but not receiving clear formulation until United States' hostility became evident after the civil war. In 1957 a milder form of commercial hostility on the part of the United States was evident from the begining. The free trade or cosmopolitan group of the nineteenth century was represented by the Continentalists in the twentieth century and these two were opposed by a fair trade or tariff group and the Nationalists respectively. In both centuries the free-trade-Continentalist group was more evident in the old, commercial capital of Montreal and the fair-trade-Nationalist group in the newer, manufacturing centre of Toronto. In the twentieth century, socialist nationalist groups of both languages, like their nineteenth-century precursors, the Grits and the Rouges, were effectively divided between Toronto and Montreal. There were, of course, important new elements present in the later instance; particularly the multi-national corporation and the civil service establishment in Ottawa. Both of these had precipitated out of the exigencies of twentieth-century technology under pressure of two world wars. In war time the bureaucracies of the corporations and of the nation states co-operated and grew through mutual support. The question was, would their different political roots and interests create a conflict between them in peace?

In this political context, then, the search for a new national policy began again. A sense of urgency was created partly by the relatively rapid growth of Russia, Europe, and Japan, and partly by the political implications of the slow rate of growth in the underdeveloped countries of the Third World. Consequent concern over growth and development on these counts did much to accelerate the revival of interest in the Innisian approach to national policy in Canada. As H.G.J. Aitken pointed out, the short-run preoccupations of the depression and the war were being put aside, and widespread interest in development was again underlining the usefulness of the staples thesis and pointing to the need for a new kind of economic theory.

Two of Innis' students, Ken Buckley and Vernon Fowke, opened the discussion by raising typically Innisian questions: to what extent was growth induced by elements other than simple staple exports and what was to be the role of the federal government in the new national policy?[1] Given the general confusion, these questions were interpreted in some quarters as an attack on the staples thesis itself; and, on some of its versions, it was. Of four general versions – a theory of development, a theory of growth, an economic interpretation of history, and an application of the traditional theory of international trade – the last was clearly removed from consideration by the questions asked. In this light it is not surprising that it was two students from the Continentalist camp who re-established the credibility of 'the staples thesis.'[2] About this same time, however, the use of input-output analysis indicated the weakness of both the new Keynesian national policy and the new Continentalist staples thesis, vindicating the Innisian position on both counts. The Keynesian analysis was too general to be of use in treating the characteristic problems of the economy; and the dominant staples industries, in Quebec at any rate, did not have the characteristics of *pôles de croissance*.[3]

---

1 K.A.H. Buckley, 'The Role of Staples Industries in Canadian Economic Development' (1958); V.C. Fowke, 'The National Policy – Old and New,' *Canadian Journal of Economics and Political Science*, 18 (1952), 271–86.
2 R.E. Caves and R. H. Holton, *The Canadian Economy: Prospect and Retrospect* (Cambridge, 1959).
3 A. Raynauld, *Croissance et structure economiques de la province de Québec* (Quebec, 1961), especially 168–87 and 276–302.

After 1963 the search for a new national policy took on stronger political tones as support for a socialist-nationalist programme emerged in the intellectual wing of the New Democratic Party. A number of the people involved, such as Abraham Rotstein, Melville Watkins, and Kari Levitt, were either students of Innis or students of students of Innis at Toronto. If Watkins can be taken as representative it is clear that Innis was not entirely understood in that quarter either; for when Watkins rejected the policy of a free market in a Keynesian framework to become a nationalist, he displayed an inadequate knowledge of Innis.

From an analytical perspective we need a theory of economic growth which effectively weds the Ricardian theory of comparative advantage with the Marxian theory of the leading role of the bourgeoisie. Given the demonstrated efficacy of the staple theory in explaining Canadian historical development, an important topic awaiting serious research is the effect of different staples in facilitating or inhibiting Canadian entrepreneurship.[4]

He was suggesting that someone had yet to do what Innis had already done. Of course there was the difference that Watkins was looking to a new national policy rather than to the old, but he evidently missed the point that the communications studies had a direct bearing on the attitude of entrepreneurs and were undertaken for that reason.

The entire community of academic economists seems to have ignored the work of the so-called later Innis. Perhaps the novelty of that contribution to the development of value theory was sufficient to prevent their grasping its significance. It is more likely, however, as I have suggested in the introduction, that that sort of value theory is no longer of any interest to them. To appraise Innis' influence in this regard, therefore, one turns to the writings of Marshall McLuhan, though there are grounds for reservations even there. On

4 M.H. Watkins, 'A New National Policy,' in T. Lloyd and J. McLeod (eds.), *Agenda 1970: Proposals for a Creative Politics* (Toronto, 1968), 165.

close examination McLuhan's work seems to be best understood only as a derivative of Innis' treatment of values and not the same thing at all.

The peculiar task to which Professor McLuhan has addressed himself is the explanation of behaviour in so far as it is controlled by the effect of technology on the way people think. He has especially given attention to oddities of behaviour consequent upon the simultaneous effect of different kinds of technology. Specifically, he has focused on the break-down of rationality when habitual attitudes and behaviour, built up in relation to obsolescent technique, are carried over into a more advanced situation. Of course this sort of thing is not new with Marshall McLuhan and has not been new since the time of Adam Smith, at least. The distinctive contribution of McLuhan, therefore, lies in the way in which he has undertaken the analysis, and it is in this respect precisely that his work is different from that of Innis, though a direct and close derivative of it.

The distinctive characteristic of McLuhan's mode of procedure is its close resemblance to the ancient, scholastic argument from fittingness. That device involves, first, the construction of a logically consistent system of elements which, for want of statement in the sources of dogma, is marred by a vacancy in some point of interest. An assertion is then made of some principle of quality which is perceived to be common throughout the system, and the missing element is filled in with what will maintain consistency. Underlying this whole process is the assumption that the elements of the system are in some sense defined by their mutual inter-relationship and that the inter-relationship constitutes the meaning of the entire formality of the system. From this it is apparent that the argument from fittingness involves what has been called an organic conception of reality and thus bears a strong family resemblance to characteristics of the more recent gestalt theory of perception. The method is, in fact, a process of rationalization in terms of some insight or creative perception, quite like the method by which one interprets much modern poetry by 'writing it himself'; and this is not surprising, since Marshall McLuhan is a professor of English literature. It can be said that his contribution to method of procedure in the social sciences is the application of a technique of literary criticism which facilitates analysis of intangible forces and exposes a different sort of causality at work in the fabric of society.

In the general run of this sort of reasoning McLuhan looks for insight to the physical characteristics of technique; particularly, because of their direct effect on modes of thought and social organization, to techniques of conveying information. Characteristics thus exposed by insight are presumed to produce corresponding characteristics in the thought patterns of people through a process of constructive impingement referred to as 'formal impact.' Here the distinctive nature of his method becomes evident.

One must remember that from the point of view of scientific method Veblen's contribution derived from his attack on the ethical vacuity of the Utilitarian school and on its consequent implicit and surreptitious reliance on final causality. He himself claimed to be concerned with the non-teleological, efficient causality of technical constraints. As I have explained in chapter two, the weakness of this position lay in the consequent necessity to consider all institutions, ideals and voluntary social movements as epiphenomena of 'blind' forces. Now it was in view of this weakness that Innis revised Veblen's method and began reconsideration of the role of values, in part as the subject of technical constraints and in part as the independent choice of personal creativity. Accordingly, one finds in Innis' work Veblen's rejection of the morally vacuous rationalist approach, his concern with efficient causality, and an additional concern with final causality. Marshall McLuhan has presented yet another revision of Veblen in his attempt to re-stress the formal aspect of the causal process.

There was considerable attention to the formal aspect of things in Innis' work, but it was submerged, and secondary to the main intent. With McLuhan it is given the first place. Innis centred attention on efficient or final causes impinging on a subject in such a way that some positive action results. Description of this process, therefore, involved a chronological recounting of a sequence of cause and effect relations. Innis was interested in historical theory, as has been noted. Focusing on formal causality, McLuhan is not primarily concerned with the existence and activity of things but with their intangible disposition or stance. This is not to say that activity is not affected by form or that McLuhan is unaware that it is, but that his primary focus in the elaboration of his argument is on the pattern or structure of behaviour, that is to say its form and the logical consistency of its form. In consequence his mode of exposition ignores the time sequence of events and turns to the juxtaposing of phenomena in such a way as to bring to the fore form, common principle, and the consequent integrity of galaxies of phenomena. Great stretches of space and time become irrelevant in his discourse. To one accustomed to thinking in terms of efficient and final causality the result seems chaotic, but in its own terms it is tightly organized in a context of formal likeness and contrast.

Nowhere does McLuhan deviate from this procedure to consider the independent role of values in social progress or the implied role of individual creativity. In this regard his work stands in great contrast to that of Innis. Innis was greatly exercised over creative liberty and its area of play within and between power centres. To the extent that he was concerned with formal analysis of the McLuhan variety it was secondary to this preoccupation. Innis was concerned with structural change and creative disequilibrium first, and with structural form only as a necessary adjunct to this. McLuhan has been concerned with 'the inevitable drive for "closure," "completion," or equilibrium which occurs both with the suppression and the extension of human sense or function.' *The Gutenburg Galaxy* is a series of historical observations of the new cultural completions ensuing upon the disturbances ...[5] Innis was concerned with disequilibrium and change whereas McLuhan's preoccupation with analysis in terms of formal causality precludes a thoroughgoing social dynamics of the Innisian sort.

It is evident that Marshall McLuhan owes much to the German tradition in social thought and that his analysis is similar to the stages theory of economic history. In fact most of the influences to which he has attributed a formative role in Innis' thinking have been more evident in his own case. Quite likely it is McLuhan, and not Innis, who should be considered the most eminent of the Chicago group of sociologists headed by Robert Park.[6]

5 H.M. McLuhan, *The Gutenburg Galaxy* (Toronto, 1962), 4.
6 H.M. McLuhan, 'Introduction,' in the 1964 re-issue of Innis, *The Bias of Communication* (1951), xiv–xvi.

What then can be said in general about the influence of Harold Innis? Certainly it has been felt in his historical works and in the work of his associates and students. His theoretical position, however, has either been misunderstood or ignored. To a great extent his work was the product of a period of adjustment in western civilization when fundamental questions were being asked and new analyses produced. In the consequent period of relative calm and prosperity that sort of thing in social science lost fashion to a more myopic view of greater pragmatic and less critical intent. Innis' place in the history of Canadian economics is secure, and others will follow him in that regard, not because they are his disciples but because the Canadian situation will in the future produce the same kind of economics that it has in the past. Quite probably some important aspects of the communications studies will continue to be misunderstood by those who have no knowledge of their roots in the nature and problems of price theory.

Bibliography

PUBLISHED WORKS OF H.A. INNIS

This section of the bibliography, with a few corrections and additions, has been taken from Jane Ward, 'The Published Works of H.A. Innis,' CJEPS, 19 (1953), 233–44. The following abbreviations have been used in this and other sections of the bibliography: AER, *American Economic Review*; AHR, *American Historical Review*; CCE, *Contributions to Canadian Economics* (University of Toronto Studies in History and Economics); CHR, *Canadian Historical Review;* CJEPS, *Canadian Journal of Economics and Political Science*; EHR, *English Historical Review*; EJ, *Economic Journal*; JEH, *Journal of Economic History*; JPE, *Journal of Political Economy*; UTQ, *University of Toronto Quarterly*.

1918
'The Economic Problems of Army Life,' *McMaster University Monthly* (Christmas), 106–9.

1921
Review: Louis Hamilton, *Canada*, CHR, 2, 299.

1923
A History of the Canadian Pacific Railway (Toronto), pp. viii, 365.
Review: W.A. Berridge, *Cycles of Unemployment in the United States, 1903–1922*; and W.T. Foster and W. Catchings, *Money, Canadian Forum*, 4, 26.
Review: G.C. Paterson, *Land Settlement in Upper Canada, 1783–1840*, CHR, 4, 63–4.

Review: W.P.M. Kennedy (ed.), *Social and Economic Conditions in the Dominion of Canada, ibid.*, 273–4.

1924

Review: A. Demangeon, *L'Empire britannique: étude de géographie coloniale*, CHR, 5, 55–6.

1925

Review: L.R. Jones and P.W. Bryan, *North America*; and J.R. Smith, *North America*, CHR, 6, 175–8.

Review: J.H.E. Secretan, *Canada's Great Highway from the First Stake to the Last Spike*; and R.G. Macbeth, *The Romance of the Canadian Pacific Railway, ibid.*, 179–80.

1926

Note: 'Rupert's Land in 1825,' CHR, 7, 302–20.

Review: L.P. Kellogg, *The French Regime in Wisconsin and the North West*, CHR, *ibid.*, 64–5.

Review: G.M. Grant, *Ocean to Ocean: Sanford Fleming's Expedition through Canada in 1872, ibid.*, 179.

Review: J. MacNaughton, *Lord Strathcona, ibid.*, 348–9.

1927

The Fur Trade of Canada (University of Toronto Studies in Economics), vol. 5, no. 1, pp. 172.

Note: 'The North West Company,' CHR, 8, 308–16.

Review: A. Shortt (ed.), *Documents Relating to Canadian Currency, Exchange and Finance during the French Period*, AER, 17, 125–6.

Review: M.I. Newbigin, *Canada, The Great River, the Lands and the Men, ibid.*, 497–8.

Review: L.C. Tombs, *The Port of Montreal, ibid.*, 510.

Review: A. G. Dalzell, *Housing in Canada, ibid.*, 730.

Review: A. Shortt (ed.), *Documents Relating to Canadian Currency, Exchange and Finance during the French Period*, CHR, 8, 62–5.

Review: C.N. Bell, *The Earliest Fur Traders on the Upper Red River and Red Lake, Minnesota, ibid.*, 497–8.

1928

'Peter Pond and the Influence of Captain James Cook on Exploration in the Interior of North America,' *Transactions of the Royal Society of Canada* (third series), vol. 22, sec. II, 131–41.

'Bibliography of Research Work,' CCE, 1, 69–85.

'A Bibliography of Publications on Canadian Economics, 1927–1928,' *ibid.*, 86–100.

Note: 'Peter Pond in 1780,' CHR, 9, 333..

Review: J.L. Burpee (ed.), *Journals and Letters of la Verendrye*, AER, 18, 97–8.

Review: J. Squair, *The Townships of Darlington and Clarke, ibid.*, 102.

Review: *Narratives of Saskatooon, 1882–1912, ibid.*, 290.

Review: H. Laureys, *La conquete des marches exterieurs, ibid.*, 302.

Review: H.I. Cowan, *British Emigration to British North America, 1783–1837, ibid.*, 338–9.

Review: J.L. Cohen, *Mothers' Allowance Legislation in Canada, ibid.*, 550.

Review: J.-N. Fauteux, *Essai sur l'industrie au Canada sous le régime français, ibid.*, 731.

Review: D.A. Heneker, The Seigniorial Regime in Canada, *ibid.*, 733.

Review: M.M. Quaife (ed.), *The Askin Papers*, vol. 1, *1747–1795, ibid.*, 737–8.

Review: H. Heaton, *A History of Trade and Commerce with Special Reference to Canada, Canadian Forum*, 8, 798.

Review: A. Mackenzie, *Voyages from Montreal*, CHR, 9, 65.

Review: W.E. Stevens, *The Northwest Fur Trade, 1763–1800, ibid.*, 65–7.

Review: F.G. Ashbrook, *Fur Farming for Profit, ibid.*, 182.

Review: L. Hamilton, *Deutschland und Canada, ibid.*, 183.

Review: J.-N. Fauteux, *Essai sur l'industrie au Canada sous le régime français, ibid.*, 259–61.

Letter to the editor on J.N. Wallace, 'The Explorer of the Finlay River in 1824,' *ibid.*, 157–60.

1929

Editor, *Select Documents in Canadian Economic History, 1497–1783*, vol. 1 (Toronto), pp. xxxiv, 581.

and A.H. Smith (translators), *The Foreign Trade of Canada*, by Henry Laureys (Toronto), pp. xiv, 325.

'Notes and Comments,' CCE, 2, 5–6.

'The Teaching of Economic History in Canada,' *ibid.*, 52–68.

'A Bibliography of Recent Publications on Canadian Economics, 1925–27, 1928–29,' *ibid.*, 98–102.

'Forest Industries in Canada,' *Pacific Affairs* (Sept.), 551–2.

'A Bibliography of Thorstein Veblen,' *Southwestern Political and Social Science Quarterly*, 10, 56–68.

Review: J.J. Heagerty, *Four Centuries of Medical History in Canada*, vols. 1 and 2, AER, 19, 161.

Review: E.S. Moore, *Canada's Mineral Resources, ibid.*, 281–2.

Review: H.L. Keenleyside, *Canada and the United States, ibid.*, 434–5.

Review: H.J. Moberly and W.B. Cameron, *When Fur Was King*, CHR, 10, 65–6.

Review: I. Bowman, *The New World: Problems in Political Geography*;
   G.J. Miller and A.E. Parkins, *Geography of North America*;
   R. Tanghe, *Géographie humaine de Montréal, ibid.*, 71–73.
Review: A.S. Morton (ed.), *The Journal of Duncan McGillivray, ibid.*,
   163–5.
Review: C.A. Vandiveer, *The Fur Trade and Early Western
   Exploration, ibid.*, 165–6.
Review: S. Greenbie, *Frontiers and the Fur Trade*; A.D.H. Smith, *John
   Jacob Astor, ibid.*, 347–8.
Review: F. Herry and L. D'Hauteserve, *Le Canada d'aujourd'hui; son
   industrie*; S.A. Cudmore, *History of the World's Commerce with
   Special Reference to Canada*; *Canada Year Book*, 1929, *ibid.*,
   349–51.

1930
*The Fur Trade in Canada: An Introduction to Canadian Economic
   History* (New Haven), pp. 444.
Peter Pond: Fur Trader and Adventurer (Toronto), pp. xi, 153.
and C.R. Fay, 'The Economic Development of Canada,' chapter xxvii
   in J.H. Rose, A.P. Newton, and E.A. Benians (eds.), *The Cambridge
   History of the British Empire*, vol. 6 (Cambridge), 657–71.
'Economics of the Hudson Bay Railway,' *Canadian Engineer* (Nov. 25).
'Hugh Allen Bart (1810–82),' *Encyclopedia of the Social Sciences*,
   vol. i, 643.
'Labrador Fish Draws Large Firms; Grows in Importance,' *Financial
   Post*, Labrador supplement (Nov. 13).
'The Hudson Bay Railway,' *Geographical Review*, 20, 1–30.
'Industrialism and Settlement in Western Canada,' *Report of
   Proceedings of the International Geographical Congress, Cambridge,
   July, 1928*, 369–76.
Review: L. Vignols, *La Mise en valeur du Canada à l'époque française
   d'après la thèse de M. P.E. Renaud*, AER, 20, 497.
Review: W.W. Swanson and P.C. Armstrong, *Wheat*; A.H. Hurst, *The
   Bread of Britain*, CHR, 11, 270–2.
Review: L.R. Freeman, *The Nearing North, ibid.*, 275.
Review: W. Malcolm, *Gold Fields of Nova Scotia, ibid.*, 275–6.
Review: L.C.A. Knowles and C.M. Knowles, *The Economic develop-
   ment of the British Overseas Empire*, *Journal of the Royal Institute
   of International Affairs*, 9, 553–4.

1931
'An Introduction to the Economic History of the Maritimes,' *Annual
   Report of the Canadian Historical Association*, 166–84.
'Notes and Comments,' CCE, 3, 5–6.
'The Engineer and the Hudson Bay Railway,' *Canadian Railway and*

Marine World (April), 224–5.

'The Jubilee of the Canadian Pacific Railway,' *Dalhousie Review*, 10, 450–55.

'Fur Trade and Industry,' *Encyclopedia of the Social Sciences*, 6, 30–6.

'Transportation as a Factor in Canadian Economic History,' *Proceedings of the Canadian Political Science Association*, 166–84.

'Government Ownership in Canada,' *Schriften des Vereins fur Sozialpolitick*, 176, 241–79.

'The Rise and Fall of the Spanish Fishery in Newfoundland,' *Transactions of the Royal Society*, third series, vol. 25, sec. II, 51–70.

Review: E. Voorhis (compiler), *Historic Forts and Trading Posts of the French Regime and of the English Fur Trading Companies*, CHR, 12, 211–2.

1932

'Notes and Comments,' CCE, 4, 5–6 and 5, 3–5.

Foreword: M.L. Bladen, 'A Bibliography of Publications on Canadian Economics,' *ibid.*, 4, 56–7.

'Economic Planning by Arbitration: The Implications of the Duff Report,' *Canadian Forum* (Dec.), 87–8.

'Economic Conditions in Canada in 1931–2,' EJ, 42, 1–16.

'Canadian Economic Conditions 1931–2, a Supplementary Note,' *ibid.*, 326–9.

'Canada Needs Trade to Pay its Debts,' *Financial Post* (July 9), 9.

Foreword: P.H. Wright, *Smoothing the Bumps in Business* (Toronto), 5–8.

Review: W.W. Swanson and P.C. Armstrong, *Wheat*; D.A. MacGibbon, *The Canadian Grain Trade*, *Canadian Forum* (June), 343–4.

Review: K.W. Porter, *John Jacob Astor: Business Man; The Reflections of Inkyo on the Great Company*, CHR, 13, 440–3.

Review: *John Jacob Astor: Business Man*, JPE, 60, 853–7.

Review: J.P. Pritchett, *The Selkirk Purchase of the Red River Valley, 1811*, North Dakota Historical Quarterly, 6, 171–3.

1933

Problems of Staple Production in Canada (Toronto), pp. xi, 124.

Editor, with A.R.M. Lower, *Select Documents in Canadian Economic History, 1783–1885*, vol. 2 (Toronto), pp. vii, 845.

'Notes and Comments,' CCE, 6, 5–6.

'The Rise and Decline of Toronto,' *Canadian Forum* (April), 251.

'Government Ownership and the Canadian Scene,' in *Canadian Problems: as Seen by Twenty Outstanding Men of Canada* (Toronto), pp. 69–90.

'The State of Economic Science in Canada,' *Commerce Journal*, 5–8.

'Sir William Mackenzie (1849-1823),' *Encyclopedia of the Social Sciences*, 10, 28–9.

'George Stephen, First Baron Mount Stephen (1829–1921),' *ibid.*, 11, 78–79.

'Interrelations between the Fur Trade of Canada and the United States,' *Mississippi Valley Historical Review*, 20, 321–32.

Review: G.R. Geiger, *The Philosophy of Henry George, Saturday Night* (Oct. 28).

1934

Editor, with A.R.W. Plumptre, *The Canadian Economy and its Problems* (Toronto, Canadian Institute of International Affairs); Introduction, 3–24; Appendix v, 'Canada and the Panama Canal,' 331–50.

Report of the Royal Commission, Provincial Economic Inquiry, Province of Nova Scotia (Halifax), pp. 236.

Contributor, *The State and Economic Life* (Paris, International Institute of Intellectual Co-operation), 252–4, 289–90.

Editorial preface: R.F. Grant, *The Canadian Atlantic Fishery* (Toronto), vii–xxi.

'Notes and Comments,' cce, 7, 5–6.

'The Drama of Canada's Development,' *Canadian Trade Abroad* (March), 6–9.

'Economic Recovery in Canada in 1933,' *Commerce Journal*.

'Contributions of the French in Canada,' *New Outlook* (July), 4, 524ff.

'Economic Nationalism,' *Papers and Proceedings of the Canadian Political Science Association for 1934*, 6, 17–31.

'An Introduction to the Economic History of Ontario from Outpost to Empire,' *Papers and Records of the Ontario Historical Society*, 30, 111–23.

'Economics for Demos,' utq, 3, 389–95.

Review: *Etudes économiques*, vol. iii, aer, 497.

Review: H.G. Moulton, *The American Transportation Problem*; M. Lowenthal, *The Investor Pays, Canadian Forum* (January).

Review: C.M. Gates (ed.), *Five Fur Traders of the Northwest*, *ibid.*, (March).

Review: J.B. Brebner, *The Explorers of North America, 1492–1806*, chr, 15, 71–2.

Review: C.O. Paullin, *Atlas of the Historical Geography of the United States, ibid.*, 86–7.

Review: H. Ingsted, *The Land of Feast and Famine*; other books on the North by M.L. Davis, J.M. Scott, E. Merrick, L. Thomas, W.H. Green, and Sir Wilfred Grenfell, *ibid.*, 320–2.

1935

'Nationalism,' Report of the chairman of the discussion group on nationalism, at the meetings of the American Economic Association, aer, 25/s, 136–9.

The Economic Basis for Canadian Civilization, Agricola Study Clubs (mimeo.).

'The Role of Intelligence: Some Further Notes,' CJEPS, 1, 280–7.

Preface: M.Q. Innis, *An Economic History of Canada* (Toronto), v–vi.

'Agriculture,' *Encyclopedia of Canada*, 1, 16–23.

'Canadian Pacific Railway,' *ibid.*, 369–74.

'Fisheries: History,' *ibid.*, 2, 342–8.

'Fur Trade,' *ibid.*, 407–11.

'Canadian Frontiers of Settlement: A Review,' *Geographical Review*, 25, 92–106.

'Notes on Problems of Adjustment in Canada,' JPE, 43, 800–7.

'Cape Breton and the French Regime,' *Transactions of the Royal Society of Canada*, third series, vol. XXIX, sec. II, 51–87.

Note: 'Some Further Material on Peter Pond,' CHR, 16, 61–4.

Review: R.G. Lounsbury, *The British Fishery at Newfoundland, 1634–1763*, AER, 25, 101.

Review: L.T. Fournier, *Railway Nationalization in Canada*, *ibid.*, 538–40.

Review: *Etudes économiques*, vol. 4, *ibid.*, 587.

Review: J.B. Tyrrell (ed.), *Journals of Samuel Herne and Philip Turnor*, AHR, 40, 524–5.

Review: W.S. Wallace (ed.), *Documents Relating to the North West Company, Canadian Forum* (July).

Review: W.C. Bethune, *Canada's Eastern Arctic*; other books on the North by 'Bob' Bartlett, G.M. Sutton, D.S. Robertson, R.H.H. Maculay, I.W. Hutchison, B. Brouillette, P.H. Godsell, J.A. Stern, and Wa-Sha-Quon-Asin (Grey Owl), CHR, 16, 196–200.

Review: R.G. Lounsbury, *The British Fishery at Newfoundland, 1634–1763*; C.B. Judah, *The North American Fisheries and British Policy to 1713, ibid.*, 326–7.

Review: D.C. Harvey (compiler), *Holland's Description of Cape Breton Island and Other Documents, ibid.*, 424–5.

Review: A. Graham (recorder), *The Golden Grindstone: the Adventures of George M. Mitchell*; other books on the North by E. Page, R.A. Bankson, B. Willoughby, W.R. Collier and E.V. Westrate, and I.W. Hutchison, *ibid.*, 438–42.

Review: M.V. Higgins, *Canadian Government Publications: a Manual for Librarians*, CJEPS, 1, 313.

1936

Settlement and the Mining Frontier, Canadian Frontiers of Settlement, vol. 9 (Toronto), pp. ix, 424.

with M.L. Jacobson, 'Agriculture and Canadian-American Trade,' sixth conference of the Institute of Pacific Relations (Yosemite, Calif.,

Aug. 1936), *Canadian Papers,* vol. 3, no. 6 (Toronto), pp. 17.

'Unused Capacity as a Factor in Canadian Economic History,' CJEPS, 2, 1–15.

'Approaches to Canadian Economic History,' *Commerce Journal,* 24–30.

'Discussion in the Social Sciences,' *Dalhousie Review,* 15, 401–13.

and B. Ratz, 'Labour,' *Encyclopedia of Canada,* 3, 353–64.

'Mining,' *ibid.,* 4, 297–305.

Review article: 'Reindeer Trek,' CHR, 17, 194–8.

Review article: 'More Books on the Canadian Far North,' *ibid.,* 413–6.

Review article: 'A Note on Recent Publications on the Fur Trade,' CJEPS, 2, 562–73.

Review article: 'For the People,' UTQ, 5, 278–87.

Review: *Etudes économiques,* vol. 5, AER, 26, 567.

1937

Foreword: Chief Trader William Gibson, 'Sir John Franklin's Last Voyage,' *Beaver* (June).

'Significant Factors in Canadian Economic Development,' CHR, 18, 374–84.

'Basic Problems of Government in Newfoundland,' CJEPS, 3, 83–5.

Editorial introduction: J.A. Ruddick, W.M. Brummond, R.E. English and J.E. Lattimer, *The Dairy Industry in Canada,* The Relations of Canada and the United States series (Toronto), pp. v–xxvi.

'Pulp and Paper Industry,' *Encyclopedia of Canada,* 5, 176–85.

Editorial introduction N.J. Ware and H.A. Logan, *Labour in Canadian-American Relations,* The Relations of Canada and the United States series (Toronto), v–xxxi.

Review: *Etudes économiques,* AER, 27, 620–1.

Review: J.B. Brebner, *The Neutral Yankees of Nova Scotia; A Marginal Colony during the Revolutionary Years,* CJEPS, 3, 610–1.

Review: B.P. Davis and C.L. Davis, *The Davis Family and the Leather Industry, 1834–1934, ibid.,* 143–4.

Letter: 'The Location of the Route of the CPR,' CHR, 18, 87–9.

1938

Editor, *Essays in Political Economy in Honour of E.J. Urwick,* Political Economy series, no. 1 (Toronto), pp. xi, 236.

Foreword: W.T. Easterbrook, *Farm Credit in Canada* (Toronto), v–viii.

Introduction: G.P. de T. Glazebrook, *A History of Transportation in Canada,* Relations of Canada and the United States series (Toronto), vii–xxi.

Editorial preface: C.H. Young, H.R.Y. Reid, and W.A. Carrothers,

The Japanese Canadians (Toronto), vii–xix.

Editorial preface: A.R.M. Lower *et al.*, *The North American Assault on the Canadian Forest*, Relations of Canada and the United States series (Toronto), vii–xviii.

'The Penetrative Powers of the Price System,' presidential address, CJEPS, 4, 299–319.

'The Passing of Political Economy,' *Commerce Journal*, 3–6.

'Economic Trends in Canadian-American Relations,' *Conference on Educational Problems in Canadian-American Relations* (Orono, Me.), 96–107.

'The Economics of Conservation,' *Geographic Review*, 28, 137–9.

Review article: 'Recent Books on the Canadian Northland and the Arctic,' CHR, 19, 191–6.

Review: H. Truchy, *La Crise des échanges internationaux*, AER, 28, 796.

Review: *Etudes économiques*, 1937, *ibid.*, 840.

Review: V.G. Setser, *The Commercial Reciprocity Policy of the United States, 1774–1829*; D.C. Masters, *The Reciprocity Treaty of 1854; Its History, Its Relation to British Colonial and Foreign Policy and to the Development of Canadian Fiscal Autonomy*, EHR, 53, 514–15.

Review: C. Schott, *Landnahme und Kolonisation in Canada am Beispiel Sudontarios*; A. Siegfried, *Canada, Weltwirtschaftliches Archiv.*, 47, 189.

1939

Foreword: S.D. Clark, *The Canadian Manufacturer's Association* (Toronto), vii–ix.

'Toronto and the Toronto Board of Trade,' *Commerce Journal*, 19–24.

'Agriculture in the Canadian Economy,' *Proceedings of the Tenth Annual Meeting of Canadian Agricultural Economics Society*, 101–2.

Preface: S.A. Saunders, *Studies in the Economy of the Maritime Provinces* (Toronto), v.

Editorial preface: G.E. Britnell, *The Wheat Economy* (Toronto), vi–xiv.

Review article: 'Recent Books on the Canadian Northland and the Arctic,' CHR, 20, 41–9.

Review: R. Dorman (compiler), *A Statutory History of the Steam and Electric Railways of Canada, 1836–1937*; L.R. Thomson, *The Canadian Railway Problem; Some Economic Aspects of Canadian Transportation and a Suggested Solution for the Railway Problem*, CJEPS, 5, 112–9.

Review: A. Loveday, J.B. Condliffe, B. Ohlin, E.F. Heckscher, and S. de Madariage, *The World's Economic Future, ibid.*, 132–3.

Review: W.Y. Elliot, E.S. May, J.W.F. Rowe, A. Skelton, and D.H.

Wallace, *International Control in the Non-Ferrous Metals*; D.H. Wallace, *Market Control in the Aluminum Industry, ibid.*, 250–3.

1940

The Cod Fisheries: The History of an International Economy, Relations of Canada and the United States series (Toronto), pp. xviii, 520.

The Diary of Alexander James McPhail (Toronto), pp. x, 289.

Foreword, C.W.M. Hart (ed.), *Essays in Sociology* (Toronto), v–viii.

Foreword: Jane McKee (ed.), *Marketing Organization and Technique* (Toronto), vii–xviii.

Note: 'The Rowell-Sirois Report,' CJEPS, 6, 562–71.

'The Necessity of Research in Marketing,' *Commerce Journal*, 12–14.

Review article: 'The Place of Land in North American Federations,' CHR, 21, 60–7.

Review article: 'Recent Books on Arctic Exploration and the Canadian Northland,' *ibid.*, 197–205.

Review: C.M. MacInnes, *A Gateway of Empire, ibid.*, 76–7.

1941

Editor, *Essays in Transportation in Honour of W.T. Jackman* (Toronto), pp. 157.

'Notes on Politics since 1918,' *Acta Victoriana* (Feb.), 6–9.

Editorial introduction: W.S. Moore, *American Influence in Canadian Mining* (Toronto), v–xvii.

Foreword: W.A. Carrothers, *The British Columbia Fisheries* (Toronto), v–xii.

'Economic Trends,' in Chester Martin (ed.), *Canada in Peace and War* (Toronto), 58–85.

'Arthur James Glazebrook,' CJEPS, 7, 92–4.

'The Commerce Course,' *Commerce Journal*, 1–2.

'Excess Capacity as a Factor in Canadian Economic History,' *Manitoba Arts Review*, 2, 55–62.

Introduction: R.H. Fleming (ed.), *Minutes of Council, Northern Department of Rupert Land, 1821–1831*, Publications of the Champlain Society, Hudson's Bay Company, series 3 (Toronto), xi–lxxvii.

Note: 'Social Sciences in the Post-war World,' CHR, 22, 118–20.

Review article: 'Recent Books on the American Arctic,' *ibid* ., 187–93.

Review: W.P. Morrell, *The Gold Rushes*, AHR, 47, 89–90.

Review: H.E. Stephenson and C. McNaught, *The Story of Advertising in Canada; A Chronicle of Fifty Years*; R.M. Hower, *The History of an Advertising Agency: N.W. Ayer and Son at Work, 1869–1939*, CJEPS, 7, 109–12.

Review: J.A. Guthrie, *The Newspaper Industry: An Economic Analysis*;

L.T. Stevenson, *The Background and Economics of American Papermaking*; C. McNaught, *Canada Gets the News*; O. Gramling, *AP: The Story of News*; H.M. Hughes, *News and the Human Interest Story, ibid.*, 578–83.

1942

'Social Sciences, Brief Survey of Recent Literature,' *Canadian Geographical Journal*, 25, ix–xi.

'Imperfect Regional Competition and Political Institutions on the North Atlantic Seaboard,' *Commerce Journal*, 21–6.

Foreword: B.S. Keirstead, *Essentials of Price Theory* (Toronto), v–viii.

'The Newspaper in Economic Development,' JEH, 2/s, 1–33.

'The Economic Aspect,' *The Wise Use of Our Resources* (Ottawa), 7–15.

Review article: 'Recent Books on the North American Arctic,' CHR, 23, 401–7.

Review article: 'Ontario and California,' UTQ, 11, 234–7.

Review: C.W. Wright, *Economic History of the United States*, CJEPS, 8, 305–7.

Review: F. Benham, *Great Britain under Protection*; W.K. Hancock, Survey of British Commonwealth Affairs, vol. 2, *Problems of Economic Policy, 1918–1939*; L. A. Mills, *British Rule in East Asia: A Study of Government and Economic Development in British Malaya and Hong Kong, ibid.*, 608–12.

Review: Y. Beriault, *Les problèmes politiques du nord canadien: le Canada et le Groenland. A qui appartient l'Archipel Arctique?, ibid.*, 624–5.

Review: E.R. Murphy, *Henry de Tonty: Fur Trader of the Mississippi*, JPE, 50, 154–5.

Review: J.A. Guthrie, *The Newsprint Paper Industry: An Economic Analysis, ibid.*, 624–5.

1943

'Decentralization and Democracy,' CJEPS, 9, 317–30.

Foreword: *Commerce Journal*, ix–x.

'A Note on the Advertising Problem,' *ibid.*, 65–6.

Foreword: M.G. Lawson, *Fur; A Study of English Mercantilism, 1700–1775* (University of Toronto Studies, History and Economics), vol. 9, vii–xx.

'Expansion of White Settlement in Canada,' in C.T. Loram and T.F. McIlwraith (eds.), *The North American Indian Today*, Part II, 'The Impact of Europe' (Toronto), 43–8.

'Some English-Canadian University Problems,' *Queen's Quarterly*, 50, 30–6.

'Liquidity Preference as a Factor in Industrial Development,' *Trans-*

actions of the Royal Society of Canada, third series, vol. 37, sec. II, 1–31 (presidential address of section II).

Review article: 'In the Tradition of Dissent,' UTQ, 13, 129–32.

Review: F.W. Howay, W.N. Sage, and H.F. Angus, *British Columbia and the United States: The North Pacific Slope from the Fur Trade to Aviation*, CHR, 24, 311–12.

Review: Q. Wright, *A Study of War*, CJEPS, 9, 593–8.

1944

Foreword: Klaus E. Knorr, *British Colonial Theories, 1570–1850* (Toronto), xi–xvi.

Foreword: Commerce Journal, ix–x.

'A Plea for the University Tradition,' *Dalhousie Review*, 24, 298–305.

'Political Economy in the Modern State,' *Proceedings of the American Philosophical Society*, 87, 323–41.

'On the Economic Significance of Culture,' *The Tasks of Economic History* (Dec.), 80–97 (presidential address).

'The Problem of Graduate Work,' *Third Annual Report of the Canadian Social Science Research Council; 1942–43* (Ottawa), 16–19; and R.G. Trotter, Letter to the Hon. W.L. Mackenzie King, *ibid.*, 21–7.

Review article: 'Recent Books on the North American Arctic,' CHR, 25, 54–60.

Review: H.F. Williamson (ed.), *The Growth of the American Economy: An Introduction to the Economic History of the United States; American Journal of Sociology*, 50, 325–6.

Review: Benjamin H. Brown, *The Tariff Reform Movement in Great Britain, 1881–1895, Annals of the American Academy of Political and Social Science*, 233, 248.

Review: E.R. Walker, *From Economic Theory to Policy*, CJEPS, 10, 106–9.

'Stephen Butler Leacock (1869–1944),' *ibid.*, 216–30.

Review: A.W. Currie, *Canadian Economic Development, ibid.*, 533.

Review: P. Kinsley, *The Chicago Tribune, its First Hundred Years*, vol. 1, *1847–1865*, JEH, 4, 100.

1945

Foreword: G.J. Wherrett and A. Moore, 'Arctic Survey,' CJEPS, 11, 48–9.

'Edward Johns Urwick, 1867–1945,' *ibid.*, 265–8.

Foreword: *Commerce Journal*, xi.

'Seeing Present Day Russia'; 'Finds Moscow a City of Gaiety and Russia Very Like Canada'; 'New, Stronger Contacts with Russia Seen Essential to New World Pattern,' *Financial Post* (Aug. 11), 9; (Aug. 18),11, 17; (Aug. 25), 11–12.

and Jan O.M. Broek, 'Geography and Nationalism: A Discussion,' *Geographical Review*, 35, 301–11.

'Democracy and the Free City,' *The Importance of Local Government in a Democracy*, Bulletin no. 84, The Citizen's Research Institute of Canada. No pagination.

'Comments on Russia,' *International Journal*, 1, 31–6.

Foreword: *Letters of William Davies, Toronto, 1854–1861*, edited with introduction and notes by W.S. Fox (Toronto), v–ix.

'The English Publishing Trade in the Eighteenth Century,' *Manitoba Arts Review*, 4, 14–24.

'The English Press in the Nineteenth Century; An Economic Approach,' UTQ, 15, 37–53.

Review: T.A. Rickard, *The Romance of Mining*, CHR, 26, 202.

Review: S. Kobre, *The Development of the Colonial Newspaper*; T.E. Dabney, *One Hundred Great Years: The Story of the Times-Picayune from its Founding to 1940*; O.G. Villard, *The Disappearing Daily: Some Chapters in American Newspaper Evolution*, JEH, 5, 129–30.

1946

and J.H. Dales, *Engineering and Society: With Special Reference to Canada*, part II (Toronto), 141–429.

Political Economy in the Modern State (Toronto), pp. xx, 270.

Foreword: *Commerce Journal*, xiii.

'Charles Norris Cochrane, 1889–1945,' CJEPS, 12, 95–7.

'The Problem of Mutual Understanding with Russia,' *Queen's Quarterly*, 53, 92–100.

'Report of the Chairman,' *Sixth Annual Report of the Canadian Social Science Research Council, 1945–46* (Ottawa), 3–5.

Review: J.F. Mansfield, *Gentlemen, The Press! Chronicles of a Crusade: Official History of the National Union of Journalists*, JEH, 6, 215–6.

Review: Eric Dardel, *Etat des pêches maritimes, sur les côtes occidentales de la France au début du XVIII siècle d'après les proces-verbaux de visite de l'inspecteur des Pêches le Masson du Parc (1723–1732)*; Eric Dardel, *La Pêche harenguière en France: étude d'histoire économique et sociale, ibid.*, 222–3.

1947

Report of the Manitoba Royal Commission on Adult Education (Winnipeg), pp. 170.

'Alexander Mackenzie, Peter Pond, David Thompson,' in *Les explorateurs célèbres* (Geneva), 154–9.

'Minerva's Owl,' *Proceedings of the Royal Society of Canada*, 1947, Appendix A, presidential address, 83–108.

'Report of the Chairman,' *Seventh Annual Report of the Canadian Social Science Research Council, 1946–47* (Ottawa), 3–7.

'The Church in Canada,' in *The Time of Healing*, twenty-second annual report of the Board of Evangelism and Social Service (Toronto), 47–54.

Review: P. Kinsley, *The Chicago Tribune: Its First Hundred Years*, vol. 2, *1865–1880*, JEH, 7, 121–2.

1948

Editor, *The Diary of Simion Perkins, 1766–1780*, with introduction and notes (Toronto), pp. xxxiv, 298, xiii.

Great Britain, The United States and Canada, Cust Foundation Lecture (Nottingham), pp. 24.

Preliminary Draft of A World Constitution by the Committee to Frame a World Constitution (Chicago), pp. 91.

Review: J. Somerville, *Soviet Philosophy: A Study of Theory and Practice, International Journal*, 3, 381–2.

1949

The Press: A Neglected Factor in the Economic History of the Twentieth Century, University of London Stamp Memorial Lecture (London), pp. 48.

'The Bias of Communication,' CJEPS, 15, 457–76.

'Between the Gold and Iron Curtain,' *Commerce Journal*, 11–3.

'Fisheries,' *Encyclopedia of Canada, Newfoundland Supplement*, 23–6.

Review: The Commission on Freedom of the Press, *A Free and Responsible Press: A General Report on Mass Communications – Newspapers, Radio, Motion Pictures, Magazines and Books*, CJEPS, 15, 265–6.

Review: P. Schrecker, *Work and History: An Essay on the Structure of Civilization, ibid.*, 266–7.

Review: P.F. Lazarsfeld and F.N. Stanton (eds.), *Communications Research 1948–49*; W. Schramm (ed.), *Communications in Modern Society: Royal Commission on the Press, 1947–1949, Report*, CJEPS, 15, 565–7.

Review: P.F. Sharp, *The Agrarian Revolt in Western Canada; A Survey Showing American Parallels*, JPE, 57, 257.

1950

Empire and Communications (Oxford), pp. 217.

A Plea for Time, sesquicentennial lectures (Fredericton), pp. 21.

Roman Law and the British Empire, sesquicentennial lectures (Fredericton), pp. 26.

and W.T. Easterbrook, 'Fundamental and Historic Elements,' chap. II in G.W. Brown (ed.), *Canada* (Berkeley), 155–64.

'William Burton Hurd (1894–1950),' CJEPS, 16, 143–4.

'Business and Government,' *Commerce Journal*, 36–9.

Review: J.M. Keynes, *Two Memoirs – Dr Melchior: A Defeated Enemy; and My Early Beliefs*, CJEPS, 16, 107–9.

1951
The Bias of Communication (Toronto), pp. x, 226.
Report of the Royal Commission on Transportation (Ottawa), pp. 307.
'Industrialism and Cultural Values,' *Papers and Proceedings of the American Economic Association*, AER, 41, 201–9.
'Technology and Public Opinion in the United States,' CJEPS, 17, 1–24.
Note: 'Communications and Archaeology,' *ibid.*, 237–40.
Review article: 'Sub Specie Temporis,' *ibid.*, 553–7.
Review: W.K. Rolph, *Henry Wise Wood of Alberta, ibid.*, 577–8.

1952
Changing Concepts of Time (Toronto), pp. vii, 133.
The Strategy of Culture (Toronto), pp. ii, 45.
'W.T. Jackman, 1871–1951,' CJEPS, 18, 201–4.
Introduction: R.M. Hutchins, *Some Questions about Education in North America*, the Marfleet Lectures (Toronto), 21–2.
and F.H. Underhill, 'Letters in Canada, 1951: Social Studies,' UTQ, 21, 281–90.
Review: *Royal Commission Studies: A Selection of Essays Prepared for the Royal Commission on National Development in the Arts, Letters and Sciences, Library Quarterly*, 22, 70–1.

1953
'The Decline in the Efficiency of Instruments Essential in Equilibrium,' AER, 43, 16–22.

1956
Essays in Canadian Economic History, ed. M.Q. Innis (Toronto), pp. 415.

SOME UNPUBLISHED WORKS OF INNIS

From papers held by the late Mrs. Innis:
'Russian Diary' (mimeo., 1945), pp. 46.
'Autobiography' (mimeo., 1952), pp. 110.

From papers held in the rare books room of the Sigmund Samuel library at the University of Toronto:
'A Defence of the Tariff' (ms., 1927–34), pp. 14.
'Economic Destiny of Canada' (ms., 1927–34), pp. 7.
'Federal-Provincial Finance in the Depression' (ms., 1927–34), pp. 4.
'Snarkov Island' ms., 1927–34), pp. 10.
'The Canadian Situation' (ms., 1940–52), pp. 9.

'Victory Loan Talk' (ms., 1940–5), pp. 30.

'The Idea File' (microfilm, 1940–52), pp. 344.

'An Uneasy Conscience,' an address delivered before the American Economic Association (mimeo., 1941–2), pp. 7.

'The Crisis in Public Opinion,' an address delivered at the 24th annual luncheon of the Canadian National Newspapers and Periodicals Association (Toronto, May 12, 1943; mimeo.), pp. 9.

'A History of Communications' (microfilm, 1945–52), pp. 1,000.

'Chicago, 1946,' a lecture on Imperial economic history, summer of 1946 (ms.), pp. 46.

'The Concept of Monopoly and Civilization,' a paper read in Paris (July 6, 1951; mimeo.), no pagination.

'Problems of Research in Canada, particularly at the University of Toronto, a talk delivered at a colloquium on research at the University of Toronto (mimeo., 1951–2), pp. 8.

SOME GENERAL REVIEWS OF, AND COMMENTS ON, INNIS' WORK

Anonymous, 'Harold Adams Innis,' *Financial Post*, 46 (Jan. 19, 1952), 6.

Bladen, V.W., W.T. Easterbrook, and J.H. Willits, 'Harold Adams Innis; 1894–1952,' AER, 43 (1953), 1–15.

Brady, A., 'Harold Adams Innis: 1894–1952,' CJEPS, 19 (1953), 87–96.

Brebner, J.B., 'Harold Adams Innis: 1894–1952,' EJ, 63 (1953), 728–33; 'Harold Adams Innis as Historian,' *Canadian Historical Association Report of the Annual Meeting* (1953), 14–24.

Buckley, K., 'The Role of Staples Industries in Canadian Economic Development,' JEH, 18 (1958), 439–50.

Cole, A.H., 'Harold Adams Innis; 1894–1952. A Memoir,' EHR, 6 (1953), 183–4.

Creighton, D.B., *Harold Adams Innis: Portrait of a Scholar* (Toronto, 1957); 'Harold Adams Innis: 1894–1952,' CHR, 33 (1952), 405–6.

Dales, J.H., 'Some Historical and Theoretical Comment on Canada's National Policies,' *Queen's Quarterly*, 71 (1964), 297–316.

Easterbrook, W.T., 'Innis and Economics,' CJEPS, 19 (1953) 291–303; 'Trends in Canadian Economic Thought,' *South Atlantic Quarterly*, 58 (1959), 91–107; 'Recent Contributions to Canadian Economic History,' JEH, 19 (1959), 76–102.

Faucher, A., 'Harold Adams Innis: 1894–1952,' *Revue de l'Université Laval*, 8 (1953), 88–95.

Fay, C.R., 'The Toronto School of Economic History,' *Economic History*, 3 (1934–37), 168–71; 'Canadian and Imperial Economic History,' CCE, 4 (1932), 42–9.

Ferguson, G.V., 'Some Memories of Harold Innis,' *Varsity Graduate*, 12 (April 1966), 73–75.

Graham, G.S., and J.B. Brebner, 'Two Tributes to Harold Innis,' *Saturday Night*, 67 (May 24, 1952), 13.

Kirkland, E.C., 'Harold Adams Innis: 1894–1952,' JEH, 13 (1953), 1.

Lower, A.R.M., 'Harold Adams Innis: 1894–1952,' *Transactions of the Royal Society of Canada*, third series, 67 (1953) 89–91.

Mackintosh, W.A., 'Innis on Canadian Economic Development,' JPE, 61 (1953), 185–94.

McGuigan, G., 'Some Remarks on the Scope and Method of Political Economy in the Writings of H.A. Innis,' an unpublished master's thesis (University of Toronto, mimeo.), pp. vii, 91.

McLuhan, H.M., 'The Later Innis,' *Queen's Quarterly*, 60 (1953), 385–74; Introduction: H.A. Innis, *The Bias of Communication* (2nd printing, Toronto, 1964), vii–xvi.

Nef, J.U., 'Shapers of the Modern Outlook: Harold Adams Innis (1894–1952),' *Canadian Forum*, 32 (1953), 224–5.

Taylor, K.W., 'Fifty Years of Canadian Economics,' CJEPS, 26 (1960), 6–18.

Ward, J., 'The Published Works of H.A. Innis,' *ibid.*, 19 (1953), 233–44.

Watkins, M.H., 'A Staple Theory of Economic Growth,' *ibid.*, 29 (1963), 141–58.

Winks, R.W., *Recent Trends and New Literature in Canadian History*, Science Centre for Teachers of History, publication no. 19 (New York), pp. 56; Foreword: H.A. Innis, *The Fur Trade in Canada* (New Haven, 1962), vii–xv.

SOME REVIEWS OF PARTICULAR BOOKS BY INNIS

A History of the Canadian Pacific Railway (Toronto, 1923).
  O.D. Skelton, CHR, 4 (1923), 179–81.
  D.A. MacGibbon, JPE, 32 (1924), 732–3.
The Fur Trade of Canada (Toronto, 1927).
  A. Shortt, CHR, 8 (1927), 351–3.
Select Documents in Canadian Economic History: 1497–1783 (Toronto, 1929)
  J.B. Brebner, AHR, 35 (1929–30), 882.
  A. Shortt, CHR, 11 (1930), 152.
The Fur Trade in Canada (Toronto, 1930).
  L.J. Burpee, AHR, 36 (1930–1), 177–8.
  H.U. Faulkner, AER, 20 (1930), 717–8.
  W.A. Mackintosh, CHR, 12 (1931), 65–7.

Select Documents in Canadian Economic History: 1783–1885
(Toronto, 1933).
   F.R. Scott, CHR, 15 (1934), 81–4.
Problems of Staple Production in Canada (Toronto, 1933).
   E.H. Blake, CHR, 14 (1933), 338–9.
   J.A. Maxwell, JPE, 42 (1934), 425–6.
Settlement and the Mining Frontier (Toronto, 1936).
   F.A. Knox, CJEPS, 2 (1936), 577–83.
   C.R. Fay, *Economic History*, 3 (1938), 98–107.
The Cod Fisheries (Toronto, 1940).
   H. Heaton, CHR, 22 (1941), 60–3.
   A.P. Usher, CJEPS, 6 (1942), 591–9.
   W.P. Morell, EHR, 57 (1942), 271–4.
   E.P. Homan, JPE, 48 (1940), 907.
Political Economy in the Modern State (Toronto, 1946).
   R.G., *Queen's Quarterly*, 54 (1947) 107–10.
   B.S. Keirstead, CJEPS, 13 (1947), 600–3.
Empire and Communications (Oxford, 1950).
   V.G. Childe, CJEPS, 17 (1951), 98–100.
   A. Maheux, CHR, 31 (1950), 322.
The Bias of Communication (Toronto, 1951).
   E.R. Adair, CHR, 33 (1952), 393–4.
   B. Berelson, JPE, 60 (1952), 364.
   K.W. Deutsch, CJEPS, 18 (1952), 389–90.
   J.U. Nef, JEH, 13 (1953), 87–9.
Changing Concepts of Time (Toronto, 1952).
   J.-C. Bonenfant, *Culture*, 14 (1953), 208–10.
   J.B. Brebner, CHR, 34 (1953), 171–3.
   A.A. Shea, *Food for Thought*, 13 (Feb. 1953), 44-5.

SELECTED ADDITIONAL WORKS

Books

Adams, Brooks, *The Law of Civilization and Decay* (New York,
   1895).
Anderson, B.M., *Social Value* (Boston, 1911).
Beard, C.R. and Beard, M.R., *The American Spirit* (New York, 1962).
Canada, *Report of the Royal Commission on Transportation* (Ottawa,
   1961).
Clark, J.B., *The Essentials of Economic Theory* (New York, 1909).
Clark, J.M., *Studies in the Economics of Overhead Costs* (Chicago,
   1923).

Cochrane, C.N., *Christianity and Classical Culture* (Toronto, 1940).

Commager, H.S., *The American Mind* (New Haven, 1959).

Conference on Canadian-American Affairs, St Lawrence University, Canton, New York, June 17–22, 1935 (Montreal, 1936).

Conference on Canadian-American Affairs, Queen's University, Kingston, Ontario, June 14–18, 1937 (Montreal, 1937).

Conference on Canadian-American Affairs, St Lawrence University, Canton, New York, June 19–22, 1939 (Montreal, 1939).

Conference on Educational Problems in Canadian-American Relations, University of Maine, Orono, Maine, June 21–23, 1938 (Orono, 1939).

Cooley, C.H., *Sociological Theory and Social Research* (New York, 1930); *Social Organization: A Study of the Larger Mind* (New York, 1929).

Donald, W.J.A., *The Canadian Iron and Steel Industry* (Boston, 1915).

Dorfman, J., *The Economic Mind in American Civilization*, vol. III (New York, 1920).

Duncan, C.S., *Marketing: Its Problems and its Materials* (New York, 1920).

Goodwin, C.D.W., *Canadian Economic Thought* (Durham, 1961).

Harrod, R.F., *The Life of John Maynard Keynes* (London, 1951).

Havelock, E.A., *The Crucifixion of Intellectual Man* (Boston, 1950).

James, William, *Pragmatism* (New York, 1963).

Knight, F.H., *The Ethics of Competition* (New York, 1935).

Marshall, L.C., C.W. Wright, and J.A. Field, *Outlines of Economics* (Chicago, 1910); *Materials for the Study of Elementary Economics* (Chicago, 1913).

Moulton, H.G., *Waterways Versus Railways* (Boston, 1912).

Pirou, G., *Les nouveaux courrants de la théorie économique aux Etats-Unis* (Paris, 1928).

Seligman, E.R.A., *The Economic Interpretation of History* (New York, 1902).

Tugwell, R.G. (ed.), *The Trend of Economics* (New York, 1924).

Veblen, T.B., *The Theory of Business Enterprise* (New York, 1904); *The Engineers and the Price System* (New York, 1921); *The Place of Science in Modern Civilization* (New York, 1919).

Wallace, W.S., *A History of the University of Toronto* (Toronto, 1927).

Articles

Bladen, V.W., 'A Journal is Born,' CJEPS:, 26 (1960), 1–5.

Donald, W.J.A., 'The Canadian Political Science Association,' JPE, 21 (1913), 762–4; 'Canadian Financial Problems,' *Ibid.*, 23 (1915),

'Factors in Canadian Industrial Development,' *Queen's Quarterly*, 20 (1912–13), 391–403.

Fay, C.R., 'Mearns and the Miramichi: An Episode in Canadian Economic History,' CHR, 4 (1923), 316–20.

Fetter, F.A., 'Price Economics and Welfare Economics,' AER, 10 (1920), 467–87; Price Economics versus Welfare Economics: Contemporary Opinion,' *Ibid.*, 719–37.

Gay, E.R., 'The Tasks of Economic History,' JEH, 1/s (1941), 9–16.

Jackson, G.E., 'Wheat and the Trade Cycle,' CHR, 3 (1922), 256–74.

Knight, F.H., 'Unemployment and Mr Keynes' Revolution in Economic Theory,' CJEPS, 3 (1937), 100–23; 'The Newer Economics and the Control of Economic Activity,' JPE, 40 (1932), 433–76.

Lower, A.R.M., 'Social Science in the Post War World,' CHR, 22, (1941), 1–13.

MacGibbon, D.A., 'The Meeting of Canadian Economists at Ottawa,' CCE, 2 (1929), 8–10.

Mackintosh, 'Economic Factors in Canadian History,' CHR, 4 (1923), 12–25; 'North America and the World Today,' *Conference on Canadian-American Affairs*, St Lawrence University, Canton, New York, June 19–22, 1939 (Montreal, 1939), 6–43.

Mavor, James, 'An Introduction to Canadian Economic History,' CCE, 1 (1928), 7–16.

Patten, S.N., 'The Reconstruction of Economic Theory,' *Annals of the American Academy of Political and Social Science*, 44/s (1912).

Rogin, L., 'Werner Sombart and the Uses of Transcendentalism,' AER, 31 (1941), 493–511.

Skelton, D.D., 'General Economic History of the Dominion: 1867–1912,' in A. Shortt and A.G. Doughty (eds.), *Canada and its Provinces* (Toronto, 1914), vol. 9, 95–274.

Urwick, E.J., 'The Role of Intelligence in the Social Process,' CJEPS, 1 (1935), 64–76.

Others

Letters, notes, memoranda, committee reports, and minutes from the H.A. Innis papers in the rare books room of the Sigmund Samuel library at the University of Toronto.

Letters and papers of H.A. Innis in the possession of the late Mrs Innis.

Appendix

Two unpublished papers

In the course of my reading I came across some unpublished manuscripts that Innis left behind. Apparently these were his notes for addresses to familiar audiences, probably students or colleagues, because they show him in a much less guarded frame of mind and indicate more clearly the intent of his argument. The two that I have chosen have been reduced to print, except for the unintelligible words which have been indicated by ellipses. The title 'Snarkov Island' is all that I could make of two words written at the top of the first page of the first manuscript. Original copies are held in the rare books collection of the University of Toronto library.

SNARKOV ISLAND

I shall warn you in the beginning that I am not sure that rent is the subject about which I am going to talk to you nor am I certain that any other term will cover the subject matter which I have in mind. Perhaps by way of introduction I should simply say that Mr Bladen and I have talked at different times about certain facts peculiar to Canada and about which we arrived at no conclusions. He suggested that I should talk to you about the same facts and present as clearly as possible some of the implications involved or some of the implications which we think are involved.

The facts about which we are concerned are very briefly the virgin natural resources of Canada and the late stage of Canada's industrial development. I shall not weary you with a description of the various

factors responsible for the severity of the impact of modern industrialism on our virgin natural resources other than to mention the more
outstanding. These include a relatively strong economic development in
the St Lawrence Valley in what is now Ontario and Quebec; a strong
centralized control of the remainder of Canada – in Western Canada
and British Columbia; a vast level stretch of country capable of producing grain with relatively slight difficulty, a mature technique making
possible rapid construction of railroads and rapid occupation of vast
stretches of virgin territory, a demand on the part of highly industrialized countries for foodstuffs – wheat in the case of England. There
might be added mines, pulp and paper, and a reference to strong
nationalistic tendencies, to a railroad built through a long stretch of
non-productive territory by which heavy overhead costs hastened production in productive territory especially as that railroad was a transcontinental line under a strong united control.

The problem of interest to the economic theorist and the economic
historian is the disposal of the profits arising from this situation. What
is the character of the profits? In the case of wheat costs of production
being lower with virgin soil it might be expected that the price of wheat
sold in the European market would decline but the evidence suggests
that the increasing industrialization of England kept par or more than
kept par with the supply of wheat, or ... more ... ... In other
words wheat rose in price after 1894. The importance of this rise in
prices was in part offset by the general rise in prices of the period but it
is probable that farming became more profitable with higher prices and
lower costs – otherwise it is more difficult to explain the marked expansion of agriculture and of immigration. Certainly costs of handling
tended to decline so far as the railroads were concerned since with the
increasing volume of traffic overhead costs declined rapidly. The marked
expansion of profits of the Canadian Pacific were in fact a result. Part
of the surplus was drained off to the hands of investors in CPR stock as
well as additions to CPR capital equipment. Substantial quantities of the
surplus were ploughed back into new capital developments either
directly as in the case of the CPR or indirectly by the reinvestment of
dividends paid to foreign stockholders in bonds to build the GTP and the
CNR. It would be necessary to follow through the disposal of CPR dividends but the tendency to regard the stock as a stable investment
probably tends to favour reinvestment of funds in capital.

Perhaps we are more interested in a theory of profits than of rent.
The gigantic scale on which capital has been poured into Canada to
undertake our transcontinental type of development has made unpredictable any definite returns. (Persuasive and persistent engineers –
Canada an example of what engineers can do. Problem of economist
to repair damage.) One of the results of the surplus arising from the

cashing in of natural resources is the speed with which capital has poured into the country and with which it has developed. Overhead costs present a continuous unpredictable situation in which mines, pulp and paper mills and power built up in a former non-traffic producing area give fresh contributions of ... To offset the increase in returns accompanying reduction of overhead costs the speed of development involves numerous extra expenditures in terms of duplication of track facilities. In any case it gives rise to a situation which is beyond the power of prediction and beyond private enterprise. This is a first result of the surplus which has arisen from virgin natural resources.

What are the results of a situation in which the profit index ceases to operate or operates too efficiently, and the engineer is allowed to run loose, so that the swiftness of the development and its unpredictable character are beyond the ordinary scope of normal economic theory? Ordinarily the results would become evident in failure of the enterprises concerned as in the case of the United States when railroad after railroad went into receivership and capital was wiped out. But the rapid gigantic character of the capital expenditure in Canada which necessitated government ownership has made that alternative impossible – if we except the case of the Grand Trunk and the Vermont Central. In the case of the Canadian National the government is committed to payment of the debt and in the case of the CPR the government is committed to payment of a practically fixed dividend rate. If the usual economic practice breaks down and we are forced to pay a high rate of interest on capital acquired through private enterprise and a low rate of interest on larger sums of capital acquired practically through government ownership without regard to earnings we become involved in the study of economic pathology. Ordinarily the capital would be paid for out of earnings or in turn from railroad rates but a young country producing raw materials for sale in a highly competitive world market is denied that alternative. Moreover our mixed railway system makes the alternative impractical.

We are forced to turn to other devices in this pathological study. Our only alternative is revenue secured from the tariff. How can we adjust the tariff so that, among other things, the interest rate to be paid on capital for building railroads will be paid by those industries which have gained from construction of railroads. This is a question more easily asked than answered. However we may suggest certain possibilities. We may confidently leave to the railways the question of ways and means of exploitation. How can we guarantee that we shall get a reasonable share of the abnormal profits which accompany the exploitation of natural resources so that we can at least pay the interest on the capital we have borrowed to construct our railways and perhaps pay off some of the mortgage. The railroads get some returns in the form of ...

for or agreements for ... construction of new branches for example to mines. The government collects a small portion in the form of royalties and licence fees, but these are far from adequate, and have the disadvantage in most cases of being collected by the provinces. Excess profits taxes or corporation taxes are notoriously unsuccessful.

The alternative is of course the tariff on machinery and equipment used for exploitation. A carefully adjusted tariff may make it possible to skim off a substantial portion of the cream by taxing equipment, raising costs of production and thereby reducing profits which would otherwise flow off into the hands of foreign investors. One comes of course immediately into the whole question of marginal plants and the possibilities of resisting more rapid exploitation on the part of the provinces by means of licences and other devices. The provinces can at least make certain that labour legislation and other legislation may be designed to prevent exploitation of labour and exploitation of resources as in the case of pulp and paper. In this case there is ample excuse for the development of a strong national feeling which will favour the investment of surplus by large companies in Canadian enterprises and the holding of stock by Canadian shareholders as in the case of the Canadian Pacific scheme to split its capital stock. Devices for increasing the prices of raw materials are seldom successful but the case of the pulp and paper trust, the wheat pool and nickel none of which are strictly comparable are instances which deserve support. Research work, education and persistent attempts to free ourselves from the persistent and dangerous tendency toward regimentation. Government ownership as a means.

It is the essence of my case that a new country, especially Canada, cannot afford to rely on the theory borrowed from old industrialized countries but she must attack with all the skill and industry she can command the task of working out a theory adapted to the situation in which she is able to defend herself against exploitation, against the drawing off of her large resources and against the violent fluctuations which are characteristic of exploitation without afterthought. Not only will such policy serve as a protection to Canada but it will also serve eventually as a protection against over ... industrialism in the highly industrialized countries.

A DEFENCE OF THE TARIFF

The following analysis proceeds on the basis of an understanding of the fundamental peculiarities of new countries and especially of Canada as distinct from highly industrialized countries. It assumes the existence of highly industrialized centres with a community capable of absorbing

a marked increase in raw materials and of supplying capital and manufactured products which make possible the marked increase in the
production of raw materials. Indeed, it assumes such an extraordinarily
rapid development of the new, economically weaker continental areas
on such a large scale that the ordinary channels of the investment of
capital through private enterprise become inadequate. The rapidity of
the development and the unpredictability of its results has occasioned
in the more recently developed areas a substantial participation on the
part of governments in the form of gifts to private enterprise, or direct
government ownership. The cumulative spread of industrialism to new
countries has been achieved largely through the support of the state.
The general trends have been evident in Canada and Australia and more
conspicuously in the latest area to come under the sweep of industrialism, namely Russia.

The enormous demand for immediate capital is inevitably linked with
the development of countries at a late stage of industrialism. Less ac-
cessible continental units with relatively indeterminate resources are
developed in relation to the demands of highly industrialized areas for
bulk raw materials. Transportation facilities for handling bulk raw
materials involve heavy initial investments which in the main have not
been available from the hands of private ownership. Government support or ownership becomes a characteristic of countries developed at a
late stage of industrialism and of industries in those countries which
demand large and immediate sums of capital.

If government support or government ownership is essential to the
economic development of new countries because of the unpredictability
of the results and the immensity of the immediate demands for capital
the effects of capital investment differ materially from the gradual
involvement of labour and capital for which economic theory is accustomed to allow in a discussion of the dynamic state. Violent swings are
set in motion according to the prediction of unpredictableness. In the
main these swings are the result of the intensified application of the
machine industry at a mature stage of technique to vast virgin natural
resources. Low cost of production is responsible for large profits and
rapid expansion. It becomes the immediate task of the government to
take advantage of the upward swings to secure returns in compensation
for the burden involved in the heavy initial outlay.

The problem may be outlined more specifically in relation to Canada.
By 1821 Canada emerged as a geographic entity engaged in the production and export of a staple commodity. The breakdown of that unity
because of the cheap transport available by the Hudson Bay route and
the strength of centralized organizations familiar to the fur trade at once
delayed the spread of industrialization and accentuated its development
when it began to take root. The St Lawrence route with the general

peculiarities of water transport had required extensive government support directly in the building of canals and indirectly in the assistance to the Grand Trunk railway as supplementary to the canals. The Canadian government had worked out as early as the 'forties and the 'fifties a device for acquiring returns for the payment of the debts incurred. The methods have been clearly described by Sir Alexander Galt. The Act of Union in 1840 had been necessary to support the extensive canal construction of the 'forties and the policy of the united governments with reference to railroads and canals was worked out by the Finance Minister. In 1859 he wrote in reply to protests from the Sheffield manufacturers against Canadian methods a detailed explanation of his policy.

It is important to note Galt's position that 'the only other course was therefore adopted and the producer has been required to pay through increased customs duties, for the vastly greater deductions he saved through the improvements referred to.' His arguments ran to the effect that the tariff was an approximation to fairness in requiring the consumer of manufactured products to pay directly in return for the lower cost of transportation for his exports and his imports. In some sense this became 'the whole explanation of the Canadian customs.' The position did not in the beginning involve government ownership. In regard to the Grand Trunk Galt wrote, 'In undertaking the construction of a railway system passing through Canada, which should connect the great lakes with the ocean, this province did not propose to effect this entirely through its own resources; the legislature only sought to offer such inducements to capitalists as might cause their attention to be directed to Canada, believing that such works as railways, the success of which is almost wholly dependent upon attention to details, were better under private management than under that of the government.' But although the inducements were sufficient to secure the construction of the Grand Trunk and the assistance was sufficient to guarantee its continuation, it was recognized that no inducement was adequate to attract private enterprise to the construction of the Intercolonial Railway. Mr Taschereau in the debates states that 'As a commercial undertaking the Inter-colonial railway presents no attractions, it offers no material for flattering prospectus, we could not invite to it the attention of European capitalists as presenting an eligible investment for their surplus funds. But for the establishing of those intimate social and commercial relations indispensable to political unity between ourselves and the sister provinces the railway is a necessity. It will therefore have to be undertaken and paid for purely as a national work.' Similarly with regard to the Prince Edward Island Railway the Minister of Railways held 'that it is not fair to expect and nobody does expect that this revenue account of the Prince Edward Island railway will ever balance. The traffic is not there and Parliament must be prepared to run the railway for the accommodation of the people and to take out of the Consolidated Revenue Fund whatever deficit there may be.'

Whatever may have been the arguments in favour of Confederation and its essential prerequisite the Intercolonial Railway, the heavy debt of the Canadas, which followed the construction of canals and the Grand Trunk Railway which had constituted Galt's *raison d'être* for the tariff, was an important consideration. Committed to a heavy debt for the improvement of transportation it became essential that new roads should be built to increase the traffic to support these facilities and the Intercolonial to the east and the Canadian Pacific Railway to the west were the logical results. Heavy government expenditure on the St Lawrence for canals and railways involved further government expenditure on the Intercolonial and on the Canadian Pacific Railway. Moreover cheap water transportation favoured a concentration of industry in the St Lawrence basin with the result that the Intercolonial tended to provide a new market for more cheaply produced Canadian goods, and a new source of supply for such important raw materials as coal carried at practically non-remunerative rates.

A characteristic feature of government construction is permanence in its initial stages and consequent heavy initial capital outlay. According to Sandford Flemming writing on July 1st, 1876, 'the railway which now connects them [the provinces] I may venture to assert will rank second to none on this continent. In the embellishment of its structures it may be surpassed by the lines of the old world but in the essentials of a railway it will when entirely completed have no superior.' Interprovincial trade was encouraged at the outset by a policy which involved low cost of operation. The results from the standpoint of Canada and of the Maritimes were significant. The interest on capital invested and the losses on operation were paid by the Dominion government necessarily from revenue derived from the tariff. The depression of the 'seventies accentuated the burden of heavy capital investments and led with the heavy commitments preceding the completion of the Intercolonial Railway in 1876 and accompanying the construction of the Canadian Pacific Railway following the terms of agreement with British Columbia in 1871 to the inauguration of the National Policy.

The effects of a high tariff served however not only as a means of obtaining additional revenue but also as an introduction of protective policy. The effects of protection involved a direct attempt to avoid the dumping of manufactured goods by the more highly industrialized United States during a period of depression on the Canadian market. But it also encouraged the trade between the Maritimes and Canada. The Maritimes began to purchase goods from Canada by rail rather than from the United States by water. Increased traffic reduced the costs of operation of the road and gave the producer of central Canada a market for his products. The deficit of the railway was therefore paid out of revenue received from the tariff which fell in turn particularly on the Maritimes as purchasers of Canadian goods. The export of coal by rail at less than cost from Nova Scotia to Quebec was an illustration of the character of exports from the Maritimes. In the problem of estimating the numerous and complicated effects of the Intercolonial Railway and the tariff the development of industry and trade in the Maritimes must be balanced against the possible losses occasioned by the shifting of the burden of the construction of the Intercolonial. It is difficult to balance the growth of industry occasioned by the establish-ment of Halifax and St John as winter ports as well as the growth of new railroad centres as at Moncton and Amherst and of new industrial centres especially dependent on land transport as the iron, coal and steel industry in the New Glasgow district and later at Sydney against the hastening of the decline of ports and of wooden shipbuilding. The increasing importance of Halifax and St John and other terminal ports was offset by the decline of numerous small ports and of wooden ships. On the other hand wooden ships were doomed inevitably by larger iron ships and small ports were bound to disappear in the face of com-petition from large ports. But the process was undoubtedly hastened by the Intercolonial. The depreciation through obsolescence was offset in part by expenditures of the Dominion government in dredging and the construction of wharves at small ports but such expenditures were to a large extent merely contributions which followed involuntary expropriation of the shipping property by the Intercolonial. Money paid out in this way was simply an addition to sums paid to the Inter-colonial to meet a deficit occasioned by paying a sufficiently low rate to attract traffic and kill the ports and shipping. Losses from depreciation through obsolescence involved the disappearance of a life dependent on the sea and involved a tremendous effort on the part of a country to build up an internal organization dependent on railroads and to shift from a large number of centres to a small number of large centres. The tragedy of the Maritimes came with the overpowering of its industry by the Intercolonial by striking at its weakest point and at its weakest moment. Revolution in transport intensified the production of certain commodities and provided new markets for such commodities as coal, fresh fish, agricultural products, apples, lumber and iron, and encour-aged industries in which the Maritimes had comparative advantages, as in such industries as wood as a raw material. But the deepening of the St Lawrence ship channel and of the St Lawrence canals proved effective in building up the industries of the St Lawrence basin which seemed to compete with ever greater effectiveness with the industries of the Maritimes. The completion of the short line from Montreal to St John in 1889 intensified the competition of Canadian goods and increased the burden of the Intercolonial. The deficit of the Intercolonial in as much as it was paid out of revenue from the tariff was borne to a large extent by the Maritimes at a time when the railway created by the tariff was responsible for extraordinary and heavy losses occasioned by depreciation through obsolescence. The burden became all the more grievous because of the period at which it was imposed and the conditions under which it was imposed.

But the effects of the National Policy involved the Western market as well as the Eastern market. The tariff was essential to provide revenue for the Canadian Pacific as well as the Intercolonial. But the tariff assumed with the National Policy a new emphasis. Formerly according to Galt's policy it was used primarily to pay for improvements in navigation and transportation. With the Intercolonial the same problem was involved but the method of payment differed. The tariff was used as a means of developing traffic as well as of securing revenue. Expenditure on transportation was met partly by sums paid by the government to meet deficits and obtained from goods entering the country and paying duties and partly by sums paid by consumers on goods not entering the country and paying railroad rates. Higher rates on manufactured goods sent to the Maritimes and lower rates on raw materials sent from the Maritimes operated to the advantage of industry in the St Lawrence basin and to the disadvantage of industry in the Maritimes. The National Policy therefore tended to shift the burden of transportation on the Maritimes. High costs of initial construction and low operation costs favoured interprovincial trade and tended to shift the burden on the payment of high continuous interest charges to be met by the tariff rather than by freight revenues. The results involved a further emphasis on tariff collected on goods imported rather than carried by rail.

From the standpoint of assistance to the construction of railways and canals the National Policy was a decided success. It provided additional revenue to pay the cash subsidy for the construction of the Canadian Pacific as well as the charges on governmentally constructed portions of the line. In a minor degree it provided a method by which the government was able to collect a certain portion of the capital brought in by the railway company, and consequently to force the company to meet in part its own charges. But this charge was in part evaded by the clause of the charter permitting the import of railway materials free. On the other hand the National Policy was effectually bolted by the monopoly clause and the opening up of the west was accompanied by a consistent and successful attempt to obtain revenue through a direct tax via the tariff on virgin natural resources and through an indirect tax which forced the movement of goods via the Canadian Pacific Railway and consequently provided for its eventual success. The alternative method of taxing involved a direct tax on natural resources or on land. The failure of the government's efforts to realize sufficient returns from the sale of land to pay the cash subsidy was an indication of the relative advantages of a tax on capital rather than on land. Indeed the attempts of the government to increase settlement were directed toward the increase of traffic and towards encouraging the protection rather than the revenue aspect of the tariff especially after 1896.

The investment of capital and the unpredictable character of its returns characteristic of Canada were shown in striking fashion after 1900. Continued investment of capital in deepening the canals and the St Lawrence ship channel accentuated the advantages of cheap water transport in the St Lawrence basin. The capture by Montreal of the wheat export traffic provided a strong pull on shipping and imports and contributed to the industrial growth of Ontario and Quebec.

Transportation improvements in Canada as related to large undertakings were followed by sudden changes in economic development. The completion of the Victoria bridge, the completion of the St John's bridge, the deepening of canals were illustrations of a phenomenon in which relatively minor links were essential to complete a change and were followed by extraordinarily rapid development. After 1900 the marked expansion of Canadian development led to new gaps in technical advance which would only be filled by government ownership. Hydroelectric power in Ontario, telephones in the prairie provinces, and municipal undertakings were evidences of the limitations of private enterprise in meeting the demands of rapid expansion. Even more conspicuous was the illustration of the railroads. The tariff which had made possible the success of the CPR provided especially with the water tight arrangement of anti-dumping legislation a rapidly increasing revenue and in addition a marked increase in earnings of the CPR. These earnings stimulated the ambition of other railway promoters and the revenue provided them with funds for satisfying the ambition. The Grand Trunk Pacific and the Canadian Northern were the result. The difficulties of these roads were followed by the eventual emergence of the Canadian National Railways.

The cumbersome character of the tariff was shown in the results – a marked development in the East, the construction of two new transcontinental lines, extremely favourable earnings for the CPR all derived largely from the impact of highly mature technique on virgin natural resources. Other weapons contributed such as the embargo on logs in 1898 and on pulpwood cut on Crown lands at a later date. The results of the tariff may be suggested in the development of the West. The burden might be wrongly regarded as the earnings of the CPR over and above the earnings of railroads placed in similar conditions. It may be doubted whether the high cost of construction of the Canadian

Pacific Railway to seaboard even over the stretch between Fort William and Ottawa involved an undue weight on the prairie provinces since the railway was needed not only for handling grain to Fort William but also for a winter route and for handling manufactured products. But the effect of rates shown in the extraordinarily high earnings after 1900 probably represented the result chiefly of skimming the cream from virgin natural resources. J.J. Hill is reported to have resigned from the CPR directorate because of the persistence in building the line north of Lake Superior but the resignation was probably as much a result of the threatened diversion of traffic from his own line which would follow this as a protest against inadvisable construction.

But the weight of CPR earnings and in turn of the tariff was not felt with any great sense of burden until during periods of depression. Agitation continued throughout the history of the road at various stages against the weight of monopoly and there followed in turn the abolition of the monopoly clause in 1888, the Crows Nest Pass agreement in 1897, the establishment of the Board of Railway Commissioners in 1903, the Canada Grain Act in 1912, the renewed application of the Crows Nest Pass agreement after the war, the building of the GTP and the CNR and their amalgamation in the Canadian National Railways, the return of the provinces resources, the completion of the Hudson Bay Railway and the accomplishment of control through the wheat pool. Finally even the seven per cent practically guaranteed under decision of the Board of Railway Commissioners appears to have lost ground with the increasing importance of dividents [sic] from other income.

But the burden during a period of depression presses down with fresh weight. A fall in the price of the basic commodity renders a fixed freight rate on the exported product a more serious burden and a higher tariff may heighten the impression of a high rate on imported commodities possibly accentuated through failure to fall with sufficient rapidity when manufacturers are protected by the tariff. World prices for a basic commodity with domestic prices for manufactured products. In the continued payment of ten per cent on increasing issues of capital and of smaller interest rates on capital for the government railways, alleged high rates of interest on bank loans, the cost and dangers of shifting to the production of livestock, the West may feel uneasily that the burden is unduly heavy. The risk may fall more sharply on the West. A high tariff ensures the movement of goods east and west and the relatively fixed railway rates plus rigid control of expenses may ensure a continuation of ten per cent for the CPR and the same circumstances a relatively slight decrease in earnings for the CNR. It ensures therefore that railway earnings shall continue to pay and that the debt may be reduced to a minimum. But it may in restricting the import of goods decrease revenue and from the imposition of new taxes such as the sales tax to meet the debt. The result is that the manufacturing community of Eastern Canada probably pays a higher percentage of the burden which may offset the advantages this section obtains from the tariff. Moreover the incurring of fresh debt to encourage construction as a remedy to unemployment has been more generally in the interests of the East. Finally the industrial advance of the East followed the rapid investment of capital in Western Canada and burdens involved in fixed capital charges shifted to the East may be more easily borne and more fairly borne by that section.

The relationship between the tariff and transportation was shown in the necessity of first providing revenue for the construction of canals and railways in the St Lawrence drainage basin. With the improvement of water transport and the heavy investment of fixed capital new markets became necessary and there followed the construction of the Intercolonial and of the Canadian Pacific Railway. The immensity of the task, the unpredictability of its results and the bargaining power of private enterprise were factors which necessitated extensive government support. Such support proved impossible without reliance on the tariff. Revenue from land proved unsatisfactory and the tariff guaranteed east west traffic by restricting imports from the south, building up industries in the east and providing revenue for construction. The unpredictability of results were shown in the expansion of the West especially after 1900 and the rapid increase in the construction of new transcontinentals anxious to share in the prosperity of the CPR, encouraged by the existence of rapidly growing revenues from the tariff and hastened by the anxiety of the West to eliminate the effects of monopoly control exercised by the CPR. The cumulative results were shown in the government construction of the National Transcontinental railway with the usual heavy initial expenditure of government construction, the completion of the Grand Trunk Pacific and the Canadian Northern as two new transcontinentals with heavy government guarantees, their eventual collapse, the shouldering of debts by the government and the formation of the Canadian National Railways. The Drayton Arworth report [sic] was essentially a Canadian product. The continuation of private enterprise favoured by Smith of the United States and by Arworth from England was overcome by the arguments of Drayton. Government ownership of the railways was a direct descendant of private enterprise and government support. The rapidity of development in the construction of railways which became possible as a result of government support and which led to government ownership led also to government ownership in other fields where private ownership proved inadequate to sudden and new demands, telephones in Western Canada and hydro electricity in Ontario.

The net result of the extraordinarily rapid development was the investment of enormous sums of capital subject to continuous payment of interest charges. Government guarantees made impossible liquidation on a large scale and the position of the CPR made necessary a guarantee from the Board of Railway Commissioners that a continuation of seven per cent was essential to Canadian financial prestige. The debts incurred during the war accentuated the burden of the fixed charges incurred with the construction of the railways. The essentially continental character of Canadian development and concentration of its transport system on the St Lawrence have necessitated centralization in its railroad, financial and other institutions. These in turn have involved heavy fixed charges from which there is little chance of escape.

The rigidity of the Canadian financial structure from the standpoint of transportation is shown in the CPR and the CNR and from the standpoint of other governmental undertakings, provincial and Dominion. The extent of the public debt is an indication of the rigidity of Canadian charges. But in contrast with the rigid character of costs the staple commodity for which the whole structure of capital equipment has been to a large extent built up namely wheat is subject to marked fluctuation. These fluctuations are in relation to quantity and to price. A decline in quantity because of seasonal variations will lead to a reduction in the earnings of the rail roads especially as the equipment has been built up to a larger extent for the handling of grain east bound and overhead charges become increasingly serious. But the effects may be less serious provided the price of wheat has been high and larger quantities of manufactured goods are purchased in western Canada with the result that returns from the hauling of westbound manufactures will be larger, industry will be stimulated in eastern Canada and revenue from the tariff will be higher; an increase in quantity will lead to an increase in earnings especially as a result of the reduction in overhead costs on equipment built up to handle grain and even with low prices but more particularly with average and high prices to a return movement of manufactured commodities with substantial returns to industrial development in eastern Canada and to a larger revenue from the tariff. Conditions may vary with poor crops and low prices at the worst to large crops and high prices at best. In other words assuming for the moment an elastic organization for the CPR the effects of a bad crop and low prices are shown for the CNR in heavy deficit and in little revenue from the tariff with which to meet the deficit. The assumption of the task of reducing unemployment on the part of the government will accentuate the deficit. The sales tax and other expedients are consequently called in to meet the situation. On the other hand the effects of a good crop and high prices are shown in a slight deficit and ample returns from the tariff with which to meet the deficit and possibly diminish certain taxes. The effect of the heavy fixed charges has been consequently to make the task of the Finance Minister extremely difficult.

The effects of the fluctuations in the West are difficult to estimate and vary with long and short run changes. But the tendency for the prices of manufactured products to decline more slowly than the prices of agricultural products in general fluctuations tends to accentuate the burden of the West. Ordinarily with high prices and a good crop the manufactured products are purchased on a large scale and the burden falls with greatest weight and is borne with least effort by the West. The point at which the tariff is sufficient to meet expenditures incidental to deficits in transportation is probably the point at which the West is forced to bear the greatest part of the burden. When the tariff becomes inadequate and it becomes necessary to resort to other taxes the burden begins to fall on the East with greater directness. The burden was carried in numerous ways. During a period of expansion with marked immigration of young skilled farmers with capital, such as came from the United States, the success of applying mature technique to virgin natural resources was such as to largely remove the feeling of burden. The investment of capital in railroad construction and in the growth of new towns alleviated the burden by stimulating railroad traffic, industry and a demand for local products. During a period of marked increase in capital investment and in new land brought under cultivation with low costs of production and relatively stable world prices the burden was noticeable only during periods of depression. But with expansion to distant and high cost lands a decline in price of wheat such as occurred after the war bears striking testimony to Marshall's description of wheat as a product elastic for a rise by inelastic for a fall. Consequently the higher cost lands can be cultivated only under conditions which involve a lower standard of living and probably losses in debts which in turn lead to losses on the part of banks and mortgage companies. Western Canada includes therefore an outer range of higher cost farms which feel immediately effects of a depression and an inner narrow range of low cost farms which feel the effects of a depression much less severely. Between these ranges the impact of the burden fluctuates in extent and intensity.